The Power of Perception

Reconstructing Your Empowered Self

Drew Taylor

The Power of Perception by Drew Taylor
Published by Perception Coaching LLC
Springdale, AR

www.myPowerOfPerception.com

This book is for educational and informational purposes only and is not intended as medical, psychological, or professional advice.
ISBN: 979-8-9869991-0-4

For information about special discounts available for bulk purchases, sales promotions, fundraising and educational needs, contact Drew Taylor at drew@myPowerOfPerception.com.

Contents

Introduction

Your perception is the most important tool you have in your journey to empowerment. Period. Yet its effects are often hidden.

Is the way you view your world holding you back?

Do you feel you are constantly at the mercy of external events in your life?

Is the world you live in filled with untrustworthy people, angry people, and scary situations?

Do those around you consistently irritate you, or does it seem like everyone around you is weak?

Have you ever wondered if you are too hard on yourself or others?

Does it feel like you're missing something...like you're playing a game without all the rules or pieces?

Life can be better. Even if the outside world stays the same, your world can change.

You may be skeptical. That's understandable. I'll make a deal with you. Simply read the rest of this introduction. If you don't connect with it, then put it back where it was and continue on with your life.

Ordinarily, when we move around in the world, we act as if it's just us and life. We act as if that's the main relationship. Life happens. It creates a reaction in us. We do something, and life reacts. Losing our job makes us depressed. We exercise, and we lose 20 pounds.

This relationship is great when it's great, except we are missing what is arguably the most important part. We're ignoring what's in the middle between us and life. What's between can make our relationship with life dark and heavy or vibrant and joyful.

That part between us and life is our perception.

Every single one of our experiences are filtered through our perception. It affects us in every moment of every day. We cannot experience life without being influenced by our perception, and yet many of us live as if our perception is fixed and unchanging, making it unworthy of evaluation. The opposite is true. It is in the awareness of our perception and the role it plays in how we experience life that we can profoundly improve our lives for the better.

What if...the solutions to all of your challenges aren't in the outside world but in your inner world?

What if...by changing the way you view your world, it could change your world?

What if...the only change needed is a change in the way you <u>experience</u> your life?

To get the most out of this book and in life, you must adopt one fundamental belief: While you can't always control the external events of your life, you can control how you experience them. That is the basis of creating empowerment through our perception.

In this book, you will:
- Gain a deeper understanding of the impact your perception has on your experience of life.

- Develop a new relationship with your perception.

- Be introduced to tools that you can use to work with your perception

- Learn to use these insights and tools to help you work directly with your beliefs, thoughts, and emotions to create empowerment in your life.

You didn't pick up this book by accident. It may have been a friend that read it and thought of you. You may be in a bookstore skimming titles. You might have found this on a friend's bookshelf or a bargain bin.

Regardless of how we were able to connect, you are in the right place at this moment.

Relationship with Life

Empowerment is about how you experience life. A truly empowering life is one where we can acknowledge and work with the relationship between us and how we experience life. This is where our perception comes in. It is with us in every moment of our lives, and it is the power within our perception that facilitates empowerment. Our most important relationship is our relationship with the way we experience life. It is within this relationship where we have the most control and potential for empowerment.

Like any relationship, we must give it acknowledgment, attention, and quality time to be healthy. Imagine how poor the quality of your relationship would be with someone you ignore every time

Our most important relationship is the relationship with the way we experience life.

you are with them. It is the same with your perception. The more you develop a relationship with it, the better your ability to work with it to improve the quality of your life.

Being disempowered is allowing the world to happen to you. Being empowered is being in control of your experience. Controlling your experience does not mean controlling the external world. Controlling your experience means digging deep enough into your own perception to figure out where it is helping you toward an empowered life and where it is getting in the way.

We cannot always shift life in our favor externally. We can, however, adjust the way we experience life to give us more joy, more empowerment, and the best experience possible within the circumstances that exist. Often, doing so ends up shifting our external circumstances for the better as well.

Empowerment does not mean we will avoid challenges in life. Challenges are a natural part of being human. It is the way we perceive them that turns challenges into either suffering or growth. Do I sound crazy? Can you picture this, or is it making no sense? Let's go deeper in!

Step Into The Arena

To start, we'll raise awareness of how your perception affects your experience. Then, we'll dig deeper into what makes up your perception and the tools and techniques that you can use in your empowerment. There will be different examples used throughout. If one doesn't connect with you at first, that's okay. There will be exercises and examples that may not make sense when you first engage with them. Lean in. Trust that it will all come together in the way you need it to.

I'll ask a favor of you. Play all-in. You already know that how much you get out of something is tied to how much you engage with it. The more you engage, the better your result. Holding back does just that, holds you back. Don't read this book like in class or on a webinar, passively observing while keeping your emotional distance.

The 'too cool', 'already know all this', or 'this doesn't apply to me' attitudes won't serve your growth. Put yourself out there. Leave nothing on the table. As Theodore Roosevelt famously said, "The credit belongs to the man who is actually in the arena, whose face is marred by dust and sweat and blood; who strives valiantly; who errs, who comes short again and again […]; who at the best knows in the end the triumph of high achievement, and who at the worst, if he fails, at least fails while daring greatly…" As you engage with this book, do it with all your being. Step into the arena. Your potential is calling.

Part One
Meeting Your Perception

Chapter 1

Choosing a Path

Sooner or later, everyone finds themselves at a point where moving forward without direction no longer works. Not because there isn't a path to take, but because the clarity of which path is ours is obscured.

"Alice: 'Would you tell me, please, which way I ought to go from here?'

The Cheshire Cat: 'That depends a good deal on where you want to get to.'

Alice: 'I don't much care where.'

The Cheshire Cat: 'Then it doesn't much matter which way you go.'

Alice: '...So long as I get somewhere.'

The Cheshire Cat: 'Oh, you're sure to do that, if only you walk long enough.'"

~ Lewis Carroll, Alice in Wonderland

This book is not about me and my experiences. It is about you and your journey to empowerment. What do I know?

I have been on this journey, so I will share the relevant parts of my path that can help you on yours. I spent enough time being disempowered to have earned the equivalent of a doctorate degree.

Growing up, I thought I had life figured out. Work hard, change the things in my external world, and happiness will follow. Except it didn't. As I began to spiral, I searched outside of myself for everything causing me to spin out. And as life does when you ask, it showed them to me. I found problem after problem and went to work on fixing them, believing it would fix me.

The first time, I thought there was some mistake. I fixed the external problem that I believed had created my inner struggle, and nothing inside of me changed. It must have been the wrong external issue.

Again, I asked what external problem was creating my suffering. I was pointed to something else. With renewed vigor, I attacked that problem until it was solved. My satisfaction dissolved when I realized that still, nothing inside of me had changed. With desperation, I frantically cycled through a pattern of identifying the external problem and throwing myself into its resolution.

The farther down that path I went, the more disillusioned I became. I wanted so badly to get away from being disempowered. Except getting away from being disempowered isn't the same thing as moving toward empowerment. The more disempowered I became, the less I had the energy to fight for my empowerment.

Gradually, and then suddenly, my experience of life became thick and heavy. As external problems would arise, I would think, "what's the point? Solving that won't give me what I'm looking for." If life wasn't the problem and couldn't be solved, then I must be the problem. Every external situation became reinforcement that I wasn't cut out for this, that I was doing it wrong. Fear and guilt went from acquaintances to constant companions.

I thought the world was judging me in every situation, and then I would judge myself for not having the courage to put myself into more of those situations. Every sales call I made added to the feeling that I was doing it wrong. Every sales call I didn't make would affirm that I wasn't enough. It was a lose-lose. Life had closed in. My comfort zone was rapidly shrinking. I leaned on anything that would ease the discomfort. I searched for something to save me from the present moment, escaping with a movie or a drink, or a song.

I searched for reasons why I had ended up in that place. I bounced back and forth between the beliefs that I was simply unfixable and that someone had done this to me.

Maybe I was just different and destined to struggle more than anyone else. No one else could relate to my problems. I was alone and isolated even in the most crowded of places, and hyper-aware in every conversation. "Does my voice sound odd? I wonder if they're judging me right now. Do they see through this facade I'm working so desperately to hold up?" It felt unsafe to let anyone see the real me.

At a certain point on the disempowered path, everything was a threat. I got to the point that I wouldn't call in a to-go order because of the discomfort. Cold calls in business made me physically ill. Social situations became opportunities for me to be exposed to myself as weak and inadequate.

Eventually, I came to an existential crossroads. I had locked myself into two choices. I could either go down the disempowered path of blaming the world, which was rapidly causing me to become more and more hostile toward it, or I could go down the path of thinking I was the problem, which was causing me to be hostile toward myself.

I had created the meaning that if the problem was within me, then all of me was the problem. It would mean I was defective and broken. At the time, I wasn't choosing to face up to the way I was relating to the world because I believed if that were the problem, it would all be my fault. I wasn't sure if I could carry the weight of that acknowledgment. What I hadn't realized yet is that the problem being within me wasn't a problem as long as the solution was also within me.

What I hadn't realized yet is that the problem being within me wasn't a problem as long as the solution was also within me.

I looked ahead down each path. The path of seeing the problem as outside of myself was darker and darker the farther down it I looked. It seemed to narrow and darken until there was no path anymore, and the air ahead had a suffocating staleness to it.

Looking down the path of seeing the problem as within me wasn't much better. I saw that if I chose this path, I would have to face the thing I was most afraid of facing...myself.

I looked back at where I had come from and saw that, on the surface, the path I'd chosen seemed easier. It was easier to blame something outside of me, instead of within me, as the cause of my struggle. It was easier to avoid what I thought was causing my suffering. It was easier to avoid the cold calls, skip social situations, and never call in a to-go order again. It was easier until it wasn't. Each new stimulus I avoided to protect myself caused my world to get a little bit smaller. It had become so small that it was squeezing the life out of me.

I was standing at a crossroads at the exact place where the sum of my decisions, and the makeup of my perception had placed me. There was pain and struggle ahead, no matter which path I chose. I saw the path of thinking the problem was outside of me would never, ever lead me to the life I was searching for. I looked down the other path and saw there was struggle ahead there, too. I'd be lying if I said I recognized it as the path of empowerment at the time. I simply saw that the path of further disempowerment was a short, dark, and hopeless one.

No matter how hard it would be to shoulder the responsibility for ending up where I had, to search within myself, and to examine my relationship with my life, this was the only path forward with any hope of the life I wanted: the life we all want.

As I began the work, I realized that the external world I perceived had changed. What had been a safe, kind, encouraging world in my childhood had turned harsh, cold, and lonely, and I had no idea why. That clearly wasn't the case for everyone else. I heard others speaking of the supporting and loving world they lived in. I saw others gaining fulfillment and success. How could it be that the world I saw, heard, and felt was different than the world of those around me?

That is when I started to discover that the world we experience has more to do with what is within us than what is without. The path to the empowerment I longed for and had been searching for out in the world was inside of me all along. I had been begging others to empower me as they passed by. By doing so, I reinforced my belief that empowerment was something I had to be given. I was a fish, desperately swimming the ocean in search of water. All the pieces I needed were already within the makeup of my perception, waiting for me to explore, disassemble, rearrange, and reconstruct them into my empowerment.

We all must make the decision on which path to take. Look back. Which path have you chosen to this point in your life? What have been the rewards? What have been the costs? As you look ahead, can you see the two paths in front of you? If you've been on the path to empowerment, let this open the way to a shortcut. If you've been on the other path, come along with me through this book. The path to empowerment is always there, no matter how far you've gone down the other. Choose possibility. Choose potential. Decide that you'll settle for nothing less than the full expression of your empowerment.

Chapter 2

Pulling Back The Curtain

The Mask

You are living your normal life as you have been for as long as you can remember. It has been a struggle, especially lately. You lost your job because a customer made you mad, and it caused you to yell at them, which got you fired. Your romantic partner made you jealous which made you controlling and they broke up with you. Your childhood made you untrusting, which caused you to struggle with developing close relationships. Life has told you that you are out-of-shape, a failure, and not good enough. Life knocked you down and then kicked you. Then, just for fun, it kept kicking you. Yesterday, life was especially rough, and after another miserable day, you fell fitfully asleep. You started to dream. You dreamt of fog clouding your vision, of something covering your eyes, and of distorted and blurry vision. You dreamt of trying hard to remove what was covering your eyes and being unable to.

The next thing you know, you are waking up in your bed. You have a strange feeling. Something is different today. You get up to brush your teeth, and as you look at yourself in the mirror, you gasp. There is a line on the side of your face from your hairline to your jaw. You touch it and feel a small gap. Panicked, you find something to conceal it and go about your day.

Throughout the day, you can't stop thinking about it. You think, "what in the world could that be?" After the day you had yesterday, maybe you finally have lost it. Trying to ignore it is too much.

You can't handle it anymore.

You go back to the mirror and run your finger along the gap again. As you do, it widens. You gently pull...and a mask identical to your face peels off. Everything else appears the same as it did a moment ago, except there's something completely different about you now.

 You think about your past. Yes, you lost your partner and your job. But now it is obvious that you pushed your partner away because of your jealousy. You chose to respond angrily to that customer, and you can see that you had other choices at that moment. It is now clear to you that you decided to push others away because of your childhood experiences, even though you could have used those experiences as lessons to help you find the right close relationships instead.

Even in losing that relationship and job, you have gained so much and grown so much. All at once, you realize a new appreciation for life. Life wasn't kicking you. All those experiences were there to prepare you for today. It brought you to the point where you were ready to discover the mask. While the experiences have been tough, you are starting to develop this curious trust that somehow, all of it is happening to serve you.

You look down at the mask in your hands and slowly bring it back into place. Everything from before comes flooding back. The feelings of inadequacy, shame, and anger are back. It was as if they had never left. You pull it off quickly.

Looking closer, you notice the mask can be adjusted. You adjust it and hesitantly put the mask back on. The inadequacy and the shame come flooding back, except the anger doesn't. Suddenly, you realize. All along, it wasn't life that was creating the sadness, the anger, or the unworthiness; it was your mask. You realize that with the right adjustments, your mask can improve your experience of life instead of taking from it.

You are not your mask. You are not your perception. You have so much power in your ability to adjust your perception. You are not your anger. You are not your feelings of inadequacy. You are always so much more than that. You must continue to remind yourself that you are not your perception. Instead, your perception is a tool that can enhance your experience of life.

You are either using it or being used by it, so you might as well choose to use it. Allow me to help you find the edge of your mask, remove it, examine it, and adjust it to help you take steps toward the most empowering life possible. This mask is your perception. In the same way you've learned to read, ride a bike, or develop skills for a job, you can learn how to work effectively with your own perception. All it takes is your commitment to learning how to work with it. This book is a how-to guide in working with your perception.

Suffering doesn't come from life directly. It comes from the way we are experiencing it, and our perception is always influencing this.

The Subjectivity of 'Reality'

For the purposes of day-to-day, ordinary consciousness, there is no 'the' reality, there is only your reality, and your perceptions are always influencing your reality.

Everything you experience in life is experienced through your perceptual filters, meaning that every time you interact with another person, two subjective realities collide – yours and theirs. Each of you has different expectations in any interaction based on your past experiences. There are unique meanings for both of you attached to things like words used, tonality, gestures, and eye movement.

For the purposes of day-to-day, ordinary consciousness, there is no 'the' reality, there is only your reality, and your perceptions are always influencing your reality.

Understanding the implications of this single idea can profoundly change your experience of life.

If you choose to ignore this, you end up interacting with others as if yours is the only view of the world, as if your perception of the world is the world. Believing the way you perceive the world is the way everyone does is a dangerous recipe for unnecessary pain and suffering. You are likely to show others love the way you want to be shown love, and only receive love if it comes the way you would express it, interpreting their actions through your filters. You might communicate in ways you would understand best, unaware of the need to adapt to their way of receiving communication. You can see how this leads to a lot of miscommunication. It is one of the greatest sources of suffering on Earth.

Imagine you live on a planet where every single person speaks a different language. Each family member, each friend, and each work colleague has their own unique language. To effectively communicate, you first must understand their language. Almost everyone on this planet realizes this and seeks to learn the languages of others and communicate with them in those languages.

Now, imagine a village of people who think their language is the only one that makes sense, and they wander through life, speaking and listening in their own language. It works decently enough, except it gets them inconsistent results. They don't understand why sometimes when speaking, the other person understands exactly what is meant and they get the outcome they are looking for, yet at other times, the outcome is the exact opposite. The person thinks, "What the heck?" I do the same thing and get different results. These people must not understand me. Why is the world so inconsistent?"

The rest of the people in the world look at this little village sympathetically, doing their best to make sense of the archaic pointing and grunting of the village's people in an attempt to communicate with them. Eventually, they must accept the sad fact that the inevitable miscommunication will always bring pain and hurt. It is no coincidence that this little village also has the highest levels of dissatisfaction with life.

When we come from a place of curiosity and seek first to understand, we can do our best to listen to others in their own individual language and speak to them in ways they will understand what we truly mean. This is the foundation of effective connection and communication.

If you've ever been around a baby learning to talk, you'll notice that most adults work hard to understand what the child's babbling means in an attempt to validate and communicate effectively with the child. The adults work so hard to understand because the lack of clear communication is obvious. As we communicate with adults, clear communication is assumed, and we make assumptions about what is meant more often. Keeping the same mentality as we have with a child and instead assuming that we don't fully understand keeps us curious and wanting to dig deeper to verify that the message sent is the message received. The lack of this is where most challenges in business and relationships originate. We should all take the same learning approach with other adults that we do with children. Never underestimate the power of effective communication, both as the person communicating and the person receiving communication.

There's a fun exercise you can do to demonstrate the nuance in meanings, even among simple words. You can do this with your partner, a close friend, or anyone you know well. Take the word 'relationship', or any word for that matter, and each write five words that come to mind when you think of the word 'relationship', then compare lists. Odds are, you won't have more than two or three of the same words. Three out of five is 60%. That would mean that if someone says the word relationship, you are missing nearly half of what they mean by it. That's how much misunderstanding is in one single word. Imagine how much assuming and guessing happens when communicating at 140 words per minute.

It's Always [Never] About You

The world does not revolve around you. Your world does revolve around you. For others, it's never about you. For you, it's always about you. When it feels like it's about someone else for you, and vice-versa, it isn't. Write these last few sentences down somewhere and come back to them periodically. Put them on your mirror, or desk at work.

To further clarify, when saying '...for you, it's always about you', I mean it is your perception, your interpretations, that are continuously involved. You are at the center of your experience, the main character. When I say, 'even when you think it's about someone else for you, it isn't', I mean that the solution to challenges

The world does not revolve around you. Your world does revolve around you. For others, it's never about you. For you, it's always about you.

for you are within your inner world and not in getting someone or something else to change in the external world.

Even when someone intentionally does something malicious to you, can you see how they are doing it to fulfill a need or desire of theirs? If someone makes fun of you, can you see their need behind it? They might not feel good enough in their own mind, so they attempt to lower you to the level they see themselves unconsciously. They might feel powerless in other areas of their life, so they feel the need to feel powerful by making fun of you.

The person making fun of someone else for trying hard or putting themselves out there is more often afraid or unwilling to acknowledge the bravery of this behavior because of what this acknowledgement would mean for them. Perhaps it could mean that they aren't as courageous, which is an idea they are unwilling to face. Therefore, they make fun of the behavior to avoid dealing with their own relationship with courage.

I'm sure you've been the person doing the judging at some point in your life. I know I have, and still have times where I do. If you look deep enough, you'll realize that your judgment had nothing to do with them and

"What is most personal is most universal."
- Carl Rogers

everything to do with you. As Carl Rogers puts it, "What is most personal is most universal." This means that when you think you're the only one with a struggle, you aren't. It also means that when you see someone struggling with something deeply personal, there's a version of that same struggle within you. Always keep in mind that your interpretation of someone else's actions is more important than the action itself.

Expectations

Our expectations are a huge factor in how we perceive a situation. Can you think of a time when something made you mad where you had no expectations in the situation?

When you've been angry, it's often because your expectations aren't being met. If your spouse or child doesn't take the trash out, and you have no expectations that they would, it doesn't bother you. If you expected them to do the dishes because you asked them three times that day to clean them, you are probably going to have an emotional reaction when they don't clean them. Our expectations either support us or hinder us. Whether the situation changes or not, our expectations can, and there is tremendous empowerment in that. Put another way, changing or dropping our expectations can change our experience of a situation, even if the situation doesn't change.

Let's look at two extreme examples. If someone punches you in the face and you get angry, it is because of your expectation of not getting punched in the face. Granted, it will still probably hurt regardless of the expectation. If a significant other cheats on you and you get angry, it is because of the expectation of them not cheating. While those are both very reasonable expectations, they serve as good examples of the role expectations play in our emotional responses.

Another tough yet very real example, death, emphasizes the difference expectations make. Take two scenarios: A young and healthy person dying, and someone dying at the age of 108. The pain and sorrow of losing someone at a young age is terrible. A lost future potential, missing out on who they might have become and what they might have done.

Contrast this with the person who dies at 108. It is often a celebration of life at these funerals, where people reminisce of the life and experiences they had. There is one key difference, expectation. The person who lives to 108 has lived 20 years beyond what anyone would have expected. On the other hand, no one expects the young to die, and that unmet expectation of a long, healthy life compounds their loss.

Expectation often gets in the way of appreciation. If you expect your child to live until at least 80 years old, can you see how you might appreciate them less in the little moments, or take them for granted? What if you drop all expectations of whether they will live until tomorrow? I bet you'd appreciate each moment with them more. I bet you'd let the little frustrations you have with them go, focus on being present with them and appreciating fully the time you have with them today. A slight shift of expectation can have a profound effect.

If you can see how expectations impact our experience in the most extreme situations it will be easier to find them elsewhere in your life. This will make it easier and easier to empower yourself through your expectations.

The practicality of having zero expectations in life is unrealistic, yet if you are going to have expectations in life, how can you have them in a way that enhances your experience?

Your expectation, as a part of your perception, will affect how much you're able to gain from a resource. If you expect to take away three key ideas from a seminar that will change your life for the better, you are more likely to do so. If you expect others are always angry, that's what you'll notice. If you expect everyone is always helpful when you need it, that's what you will often receive.

What are your expectations of this book?

We've already looked at several key things that you could choose to take away. Simply the awareness that your perception exists and what it is made of will improve your life. Understanding the impact your perception has on your experience of life will further that improvement. Developing a new relationship with your perception and using tools to work directly with it will take your life to a level of empowerment you have never experienced before.

Developing a new relationship with your perception and using tools to work directly with it will take your life to a level of empowerment you have never experienced before.

This isn't *a* resource; it is *your* resource.

Before we move on, write down your expectations for what you'll gain from engaging with The Power of Perception.

I expect this book to

_____

_____

As a side note, please *do* write in this book. It is a place to record where you are now, the positive changes that come throughout the book, and it will be here to reflect back on and see how you've grown later!

Chapter 3

Barriers to Empowerment

As with any meaningful endeavor in life, there are barriers to overcome along the way. Being human, we tend to get in our own way more often than others get in our way. Since we get in our way, the great news is that we can also get out of our way. As we develop a heightened awareness of these barriers, it begins to loosen them.

We'll start with some perceptual barriers on the path to empowerment, dig into each of them, and prepare ourselves to face them head-on. You'll gain more awareness and momentum toward empowerment as we work through them.

Before we get to the barriers to empowerment, it's helpful to first define empowerment.

Merriam-Webster defines empowerment as "the act or action of empowering someone or something : the granting of the power, right, or authority to perform various acts or duties". It also defines it as "the state of being empowered to do something : the power, right, or authority to do something."

The first definition implies that the power or authority is granted, that it comes from outside of ourselves. This is exactly how most of us grow up to understand empowerment. We wait to be granted empowerment. We look to a boss, or a parent, or whatever authority figure we have placed in our life. We hope and wait for them to grant this empowerment to us. We define it as caused by something outside of ourselves. We put ourselves at-effect and wish for it to happen to us.

If we're proactive, we read books, go to seminars, or hire life and business coaches. The tricky part is that, on the surface, it looks the same for different people using the same resource. One of them is empowering themselves with it and the other is further disempowering themselves.

The difference is subtle. If there's a hint of seeking a savior in it, it disempowers. If it's the book, or the seminar, or the coach that solved the challenges, it further disempowers. The line is so fine that it requires constant reflection to notice which is happening.

With time, luck, or the right resource, we start to see it all clearly. As the veil lifts and we finally see behind the curtain, we find that it was actually us that took our own empowerment and handed it to someone else. Hiding our innate authority from ourselves, we projected it out and gave it to whichever authority figure fit us. We then lived our life seeking the right genie that would grant empowerment to us, or we raged against the machine of the authority we unconsciously chose. All the while, we continued pretending that the empowerment that had always been ours was somehow in the control of someone or something external.

Maybe it's because our own power was too scary, that we didn't trust ourselves with it, or that we didn't feel like we deserved it. Maybe because everything else in life seemed conditional, we had to unconsciously make our empowerment the same.

That brings us to the second definition of empowerment, "the state of being empowered to do something". This is the one we will use for this book. Being empowered is not "doing" empowered. Being implies it is within our identity, that the empowerment is innate. The state of being empowered implies that it is a state we can move into or out of, but is always available. Like a light switch we can turn on or off.

If it is an internal state and an innate part of our being, then what we are really seeking when seeking empowerment is to be able to find the switch within. We are seeking to find the controls for empowerment that is within us. We are seeking to see the barriers to our empowerment clearly enough to be able to remove them, knowing that when those barriers are removed, what's left is our natural empowerment that we hid from ourselves all those years ago.

That's the aim of this book. It isn't about gifting you empowerment. I am not your savior, and I don't have the power to do that. You are your own savior using the resource of this book to become consciously clear of all the creative ways you have hid your empowerment from yourself. As you do so, you'll experience again what you are and have always been beneath the surface, your empowered self.

Let's now look at each of these barriers.

Resistance

Resistance is one of the things that hold us back from our potential. It creates drag, like a boat attempting to drive away with the anchor down. Paying attention to our resistance can help us better understand ourselves and attain more of what we want in life.

Inner resistance can be subtle. Notice if any of these examples connect with you. Resistance can show up as:

- "I don't have enough money."

- "They aren't qualified enough to teach me."

- "I've already heard that before."

- "That is too complicated for me."

- "I'm afraid of what will happen if I buy into this."

- "Nothing else worked, so why would this?"

- "This is stupid."

- "I'm too busy."

Resistance can be subtle or overt.

Paying attention to resistance can uncover a trigger for you. In the context of this book, a trigger means something that is causing a response that is out of proportion to the event. Triggers are guides directing you to the areas within that can benefit most from inner work.

How do you tell if resistance is showing up for you in the form of a trigger? We'll clarify with an example. If someone punches you in the face and you get upset, it is a response proportional to the event. It is a reasonable response to getting punched. If someone tells you they aren't interested in

Triggers are guides directing you to the areas within that can benefit most from inner work.

what you are selling and that throws you into a shame cycle that ends with you curled up in a ball on the floor, it is a response out of proportion to the event.

These out-of-proportion responses can guide us back to disempowering beliefs or emotional baggage. These beliefs often affect us elsewhere in life, too. By uncovering them, you'll open to the possibility of letting them go and improving the quality of your life.

We all experience resistance at times in our lives. For me, resistance has shown up in the forms of "I'll be just fine without it", "what happens if I fail?" and "that's not a good use of my time." Left alone, that resistance would have cost me my entire growth journey to this point. It would have made me miss out on some of the most enriching experiences of my life. It would have cost me so much of the empowerment I've gained from continuing to take leaps of faith into my own vulnerability.

If you experience resistance as you read this book, celebrate it. It is there to teach you something. It is opening an opportunity for healing and growth you were previously unaware of. In writing this book, I aim to pull resistances within you into the light so we can examine them through new eyes.

Why might resistance show up for you while reading this book? If you've always had the power to change an aspect of your life for the better, and only now you become aware of that through engaging with this book, would it mean that it was somehow 'your fault' that you hadn't changed it sooner?

Is shame, fear, or another disempowering emotion creating resistance for you? Maybe your go-to resistance is, "that's great, but these kinds of things don't work for me." Perhaps you go with, "I don't trust you enough to try this." It's natural for those kinds of beliefs and emotions to surface at times. When they surface through your reading, write them down, then come back to wherever you are in the book. You'll find techniques to unravel them as you read further.

Secondary Gain

Another reason resistance might appear while reading this book is called 'secondary gain.' Secondary gain is when a problem or challenge comes with a secondary benefit, where we associate letting go of the problem with having to let go of the gain.

Someone who gets a lot of attention because of their problems is a good example of this. The connection can be made in this person's mind, which says, "If I have problems, I get attention." The gain that comes with the problems is attention. They might have made the association that if they give up the problems, they will have to give up the attention. When they want to let go of the problems, they will have to resolve the 'secondary gain' and figure out how to get the attention differently while still letting go of the problems.

If you consciously want to change, yet still feel resistance, 'secondary gain' might be involved. This 'secondary gain' has the power to keep you holding on to something that is causing you pain. Not addressing and resolving 'secondary gain' will keep you in a state of frustration and get in the way of your empowerment.

The tricky part is that the gain doesn't have to make sense consciously. For example, you may have an issue with getting angry over small things. It may have caused damage to your relationships and created problems for you. Yet, if being angry makes you feel in control of your life, then you might equate letting go of the anger to letting go of that feeling of control.

To let go of the 'secondary gain', we must acknowledge that either the gain isn't worth holding onto the problem or that we can get the gain in another way that doesn't require us to keep the problem. If you notice resistance coming up for you, write or say out loud the answer to the questions below. If you aren't feeling any resistance working through this book, think of another area in your life where you are resisting, and insert that instead.

To let go of the 'secondary gain', we must acknowledge that either the gain isn't worth holding onto the problem or that we can get the gain in another way that doesn't require us to keep the problem.

What do you gain by resisting (this book)?

What do you lose by resisting (this book)?

What do you gain by not resisting (this book)?

What do you lose by not resisting (this book)?

This book can help you take back control of your empowerment. If your 'secondary gain' has been comfort, if your limiting beliefs have kept you safe, if disempowering emotions have held you back from taking positive risks, you can overcome these. You can decide to let go of the problem and still enjoy comfort, safety, and protection. Ask yourself if there is a better way to get the same result, and you'll realize there always is.

Look in the mirror and tell yourself that deciding to read the entirety of this book is taking the next step in your empowerment. When you reflect on this decision, you'll remember that you chose empowerment and that no one else could have chosen it for you.

Choosing to face your fears, your demons, and your disempowering beliefs by acknowledging and changing them will serve you in gaining fulfillment and fulfilling your potential.

Lack of Power to Effect Change

Another barrier to empowerment is disbelieving that you can change. In the Cause-and-Effect reality we live in, we either fall more on the Cause side or more on the Effect side. If we want to find the fastest way to misery, we can start spending our time on the Effect side, more commonly known as 'being a victim,' which, fittingly, has a lot of negativity attached.

If your life is happening to you without any personal input, then life does whatever it wants to you, and you're merely a victim of your circumstances. This way of thinking tends to create feelings of powerlessness and futility. What's the point of trying if we don't have any control and life isn't on our side?

I won't sugarcoat it. Retraining ourselves to be 'at Cause' can be very painful for a short period of time. However, remaining 'at Effect' to life is the path of never-ending suffering. If the choice was between a band-aid being ripped off or a band-aid being endlessly peeled away throughout your lifetime, which would you choose?

Choosing to be 'at Cause' in your life is one of the key decisions you must make to step into empowerment. You might still need clarification on what being 'at Cause' means or how to do it. The remainder of this book will clarify what being 'at Cause' means and also serves as a how-to guide.

Above Examination

Before we get too far into the exercises, we must examine two more potential barriers to our empowerment. The first can be one of the most sensitive subjects because it is the source of some of the most deeply held beliefs: religion and spirituality. Our deep-seated beliefs can have a profound effect on our ability to change. With their roots in childhood, family, and society, they can be a huge help or a formidable barrier to positive change.

Religious and spiritual beliefs are areas many of us may feel a deep resistance to examining, as if we are doing something wrong by examining them at all. The choice is ultimately yours as the reader. Before passing on this section, remember that being unaware of any barriers to your empowerment will likely hold you back from your greatest potential, fulfillment, and positive impact on the world.

If this section creates any discomfort, please do two things. First, forgive me. I don't want you to miss out on an opportunity to improve your life. Secondly, look back at the section on resistance. Are you unwittingly putting up a barrier? Just know that if you do choose to pass over this section, you may miss out on the very resource that could help you take the biggest step forward in your empowerment.

At the risk of restating the obvious, what you believe about spirituality, God, or the higher power in your life strongly influences your perception and your life. Spirituality and religion play a huge role in developing our beliefs and values. Even if you don't identify as spiritual or religious, many aspects of our societies and cultures are heavily influenced by spirituality and religion, so they have still influenced you. These influences can be wonderful for empowerment, purpose, joy, and a meaningful life.

The question to ask yourself is whether you have ever felt that your human nature is bad, that you shouldn't express your anger, that you should feel shameful when you aren't grateful, or that suffering should go hand in hand with being spiritual. There is a whole host of possible misinterpretations. If any of those connect with you, be mindful that a misunderstanding of your spiritual beliefs might be at the heart of it.

If that is the case, as with every other barrier to empowerment, I urge you to treat it the same. Challenge the resistance. Challenging your beliefs and interpretation of the teachings of your religion is not turning your back on it or disrespecting it. It is finding the understanding of it through which you can give yourself the love, worth, and beliefs that will cause you to show up as a light in the world. Which, in fact, is in perfect alignment with most religions.

Let's look first at Spiritual Bypassing. Spiritual Bypassing is a term coined by John Welwood, a psychotherapist and author. He has described it as a "tendency to use spiritual ideas and practices to sidestep or avoid facing unresolved emotional issues, psychological wounds, and unfinished developmental tasks."

There can be a complicated dichotomy in any religion. On the one hand, there is the focus on leaning into faith, where our experiences are designed for us to grow and evolve and where we can transcend our programming. On the other hand, our spirituality can help us focus on what limits us and face it head-on to align more with what we want in our lives. There is a delicate balance between these, and they can be viewed in a way that they support each other instead of being in conflict.

If you are inadvertently using your spirituality to avoid any of these, you can start to empower yourself by realizing that it isn't an either/or. You don't have to choose to either embrace your spirituality or face unresolved issues. You can be highly spiritual while addressing them directly. You can start to bring some of them to the surface for resolution.

Use the following examples to help you identify anything you could be avoiding through Spiritual Bypassing. Then, take a moment and write down anything that comes to mind that you could be avoiding.

- I avoid and ignore my anger because I believe that feeling or expressing anger isn't appropriate in my religion.

- I feel inadequate, yet I choose to avoid facing those feelings directly and instead lean into my spiritual practices.

- I and my nature are inherently bad so I must do good things to counteract this and become worthy.

_____

_____

_____

It is one thing to challenge religion or spirituality directly. Examining our *interpretations* of our religion or spirituality is entirely different, which is exactly what I am proposing. Here's an example from myself.

My misinterpretation of the religious teachings I grew up with was that through acts of good and accomplishments, I could earn worth. The belief that developed was, "If I do enough good things, it will balance out that I am inherently bad and without worth." This belief wasn't the actual teaching of my religion; it was my misinterpretation. It took me decades to become aware of the belief. It took me a while longer to develop the courage to examine the source of the belief and realize that I had it backward for my empowerment. It wasn't because I was unworthy that I needed to do good things. How good could my good deeds be if they were all done to escape being inherently bad?

Through examination, I was able to turn that disempowering belief around. I realized that I do good things because I am unconditionally worthy and that love and positive action are natural byproducts of unconditional worth. It was a small shift with profound effects. I had misinterpreted the religious teachings, creating a disempowering belief that was the undercurrent of the narrative of my life.

Part of my reluctance to examine this earlier belief was that it fell under the umbrella of religion. I had decided that it would be sacrilegious to examine this belief because by examining the belief, I would be directly challenging my religion. I had placed this belief into a box and labeled it 'above examination'. Had I left it there, it would have continued to contribute to endless pain and suffering throughout my life. This is not to say religious or spiritual groups are teaching bad beliefs, but that we can take on beliefs from anywhere. And any area we refuse to examine can be dangerous to our empowerment.

Take a moment and think about the beliefs you developed in your religious or spiritual environment. Examine how they relate to your experience of life. Have you accidentally taken on beliefs limiting your joy, love, or worth? Open this box, even if it was previously a box that was 'above examination,' and write down any beliefs you have misinterpreted that are causing disempowerment in your life. The goal of this exercise is to simply open the box and become aware without attaching meaning to the new awareness.

_____

_____

_____

_____

"I'm aware," you say. Now what? The beautiful thing about this entire book and the process of change is that awareness is the first step. In many cases, it is the only step. If you continue to remain aware, awareness can start an unconscious process of unraveling the problem. Awareness can be like knocking over the first domino. You will go through exercises later in the book to help you work with what you've uncovered.

> *If you continue to remain aware, awareness can start an unconscious process of unraveling the problem.*

Chapter 4

Influences on our Perception

The Puppet Master

Here I am again, being jerked around by my strings. The Puppet Master gets angry, and it forces me to feel angry. My anger automatically makes me feel guilty. He calls me weak and tells me I think too much and am selfish. He's tugging on the strings of my shame, and I convulse. I crawl back into the hole I came from because that's where I belong. The phone rings and makes me feel even worse. The threat on the other end of the line is going to make me feel terrible. Maybe I'll hide here because it feels safer. I don't have any control over any of this anyway. I'm too emotional, too sensitive, too tired, and too weak.

All these things that are happening to me are unfair. Well, maybe they are fair because I'm weak and bad. I deserve this. I'm not enough. I'm never enough. Now I see threats everywhere. I'm a balloon in a world of needles. I'm a feather being blown this way and that in the wind. I'm the puppet. I strain against the strings. I pull with all my might, gnawing at them with my teeth, screaming until I'm red-faced, breathless, and sobbing. It's no use. I stop struggling and give in. He can do what he will with me. I can't go on like this. It's time to face my perpetrator and get it over with.

At that moment, the strings go slack and fall to the floor. I follow them, knowing I'll find the puppet master there. It's dark. All I see is his outline at the far side of the room. I ease closer, preparing to be jerked around again. He's right in front of me, but he looks different.

He looks…familiar.

There's a light switch next to me on the wall, and I flip it. Here I am, face to face with the Puppet Master, and that's when I remember. He and I are one… there was only me all along.

And as you notice…

that the one who is doing…

and the one who feels done to…

are, in a deeper way…

the same…

You may begin to sense…

a little more space inside…

Space where a different kind of power can enter…

You…

as both the cause…

and the effect…

And as you allow yourself…

to simply allow…

You might notice a quiet sense of choice emerging…

Behind judgment…

beneath fear…

Beyond the push and pull of cause and effect…

Is you.

Have you ever been called a Puppet before? It's offensive, isn't it? If you take offense, that's good. It means you are becoming aware and taking control. Follow the hurt, follow the anger. It will lead you back to the source of it and offer an opportunity for resolution, for an increase in wholeness.

Let's stop and examine your assumptions of the statement "you are a puppet." What if I said you were also the puppet master? Does that change things? Being a puppet is only a problem if you aren't the one controlling the strings. While your beliefs and emotions can be in control of you, you also have the power to influence and guide them. So, you can't control yourself but you can control what controls you. Odd and counterintuitive, I know. Such is the nature of working with the unconscious. This empowerment is yours to take back.

Let's look at one last barrier to empowerment before we get to work on your perception.

Being a puppet is only a problem if you aren't the one controlling the strings.

Beliefs about Positive Change

The subject of positive change is a confusing one. Some people say it takes decades to change, some say it takes 21 days, and some say it happens in an instant. What do you say? What are the implications of your belief if you feel it takes decades to change? The good news is that change can and does happen in an instant. I'll prove it.

Think of the last thing you changed in your life for the better. How long did that change truly take? You may be partially correct if you say it took years. We must separate the process of being ready for the change from the actual moment of change, as it is the preparation for change that may have taken years. The actual moment of change comes in the moment of the decision. It comes in an instant. We've all heard it, time and time again, that moment when someone finally says, "that's enough." From that moment forward, they are never the same.

The good news is that if we are prepared to stay open and aware of the potential for change and drop our resistance, positive change will come quicker and quicker to us.

We must separate the process of being ready for the change from the actual moment of change, as it is the preparation for change that may have taken years.

There's a popular story about the lion who came upon a flock of sheep, only to find a lion amongst the sheep. It was a lion who'd been raised by the sheep since he was a cub. It would eat grass like a sheep, bleat like a sheep, and move like a sheep. The lion that came upon the flock roared, and all of the sheep trembled. When the sheep-lion stood in front of the lion, it cowered.

The lion said, "What are you doing with these sheep?"

The sheep-lion said, "Please don't eat me. I am a sheep."

"No, you are a lion," said the Lion.

"Yes, I am whatever you say; just please don't eat me," replied the sheep-lion.

Realizing the sheep-lion did not believe him, the lion dragged him to a pool of water and said, "Look!"

When the sheep-lion looked at his reflection in the water, he let out a roar, and at that moment, he was forever transformed.

Just like the sheep-lion, transformation happens in moments when we are truly aware of what and who we are.

Judging by Actions vs. Intentions

It is said that we judge ourselves by our intentions and others by their actions. Have you ever thought about doing the opposite? Doing so will increase your understanding, compassion, and communication. Pay attention to your actions and how they may be perceived. Are they different from how you intended? Pay attention to the positive intention behind others' actions because there will always be one. It may be hidden underneath layers and layers of strange logic, yet it's there.

The moment we write someone off based on their actions, we lose our ability to understand the human. Are they unintentionally acting in a way that manifests itself more negatively than intended?

Think of school children. What does the little girl who likes the boy do when she has a crush? She is mean, bosses him, and picks on him. She has good intentions, yet he judges her actions. He gets upset, even though the intention behind her action is positive. You might think we naturally grow out of that as adults. We don't.

It could be said that most challenges between people are due to misunderstandings. What would our experience of living be like if, instead, we always believed the best about others and judged them by their intentions? What if we looked at someone else and believed that behind their unfavorable behaviors were good intentions? What if we considered every poor behavior as a less than ideal expression of a positive intention?

On a certain level, doesn't everyone want the same things? To be loved, to be enough, to connect with others, to succeed, to have freedom?

What if we considered every poor behavior as a less than ideal expression of a positive intention?

Everyone wants to be loved. Some people become codependent and clingy because they believe it's the best way to get that love. Some people push others away and constantly test those around them because they believe it's the best way to get proof and confirmation that they are loved. It's a beautiful and universal intention to be loved. It's only the expression of that intention that can be problematic.

What if we all looked at the whole world through that lens? How much more understanding and compassionate would that allow us to be on a daily basis?

That decision is three seconds away. We can change our entire experience of life in three seconds. A small change with a profound effect.

The following exercise will help us to see the world through this lens.

- Think back to the last three times you were hurt, upset, or frustrated by someone else. Write them down.

- Write what their positive intention might have been.

Put it all together in this format:

"The way they attempted to express (positive intention) was (the action they took). They were taking the best approach to getting (positive intention) that they knew at the time."

_____

_____

Example:

My boss yelled at me when I messed up on a customer proposal at work.

Her positive intention might have been that (she believed I am capable of more).

The way she attempted to express (her belief that I am capable of more) was (to yell at me). She was taking the best approach to getting (me to step into my potential) that she knew at the time.

Decide to experience this positive change. Spend the next week looking for the others' positive intentions in your interactions. I guarantee you will feel better.

Person vs. Object

Seeing others as a person or an object is a subtle shift we all make from time to time. Shifting someone from a person to an object always includes a label. A label is anything used to describe someone or a box they can be put in. 'Salesperson' and 'jock' are both examples of labels. Often, when we label someone, it turns them into an object to us, such as a 'cop,' 'gang member,' or 'politician.' These labels separate us from them, making it easier to judge, generalize, ignore, or treat them poorly because we have dehumanized them.

If everyone in your world starts becoming an object, your world will become cold and detached. This can be a miserable place to be, making it impossible to understand and connect positively with others.

Business, sales, and overall relationship success are based on the ability to change yourself from being an object in someone else's mind to being a human.

People don't buy products or services they want from objects; they buy them from humans they connect with. People don't develop deep, emotional connections with objects (all jokes aside). They develop connections with other people. In the same

> *Business, sales, and overall relationship success are based on the ability to change yourself from being an object in someone else's mind to being a human.*

way, objects aren't very receptive to a sales pitch or a conversation. They are, however, receptive to someone who understands their current situation and how the product or service can help them get what they want.

See if you can feel it when you do it.

When do you see others as people, and when do they shift to objects or vice versa? When you think of those IRS auditors or those telemarketers, are they people or objects? And what happens when you think of someone you know well who happens to be a telemarketer? You know their family, likes, dislikes, fears, and aspirations. You know why they have the job and who they are outside that role. Now, are they still an object, or have they become a person? When you see someone as an object, how do you think about or act toward them?

Let's go deeper into this with the telemarketer. The telemarketer that calls is a human being. Let's give her the name of someone you are close with. Let's imagine she has three kids and a family, which she supports by showing up to work twelve hours a day in a call center. She is so much more than the label of 'telemarketer.'

It is easy to reject or be rude or angry toward someone you feel is interrupting your day, and without invitation. It is harder to be that way toward [Sharon], who rides a train or a bus and then walks twenty minutes both ways to get to a job where people threaten her or yell at her for the majority of the day. She tries to smile her way through because she knows that this job is helping to feed her children.

Imagining all of this will make us more patient and empathetic. No one is saying we have to buy the vacuum when someone calls us at 7 PM on a Sunday selling them. Yet we might end the call with, "I don't want to waste your time as I won't be buying a vacuum. I wish you success with your next calls," instead of telling them they should be ashamed for calling late on a weekend night.

Looking at another place this commonly shows up, social media, we can understand the difference between seeing someone as a person or an object even better.

How is it that people can be so mean online when they aren't nearly as aggressive in person? Well, it's harder to turn people into objects if they are right in front of you and can see you and humanize themselves. It's much easier to say hateful things when you can objectify the person you are attacking as 'one of those influencers,' or 'that person representing the political party I don't like.'

If you are on the receiving end of this, keep in mind that what they are attacking is the object you represent in their mind, not you. You can protect yourself emotionally from rejection or judgment by realizing that you aren't what they are rejecting, but rather, the object you represent.

To feel rejection, you must then take what they said and internalize it. In that way, only you can reject yourself. No one can make you feel rejected without your permission.

Shifting yourself in the eyes of others, from being an object to being a person, can be tricky. You must break out of their label for you. 'Humanizing yourself,' or behaving in a way that doesn't fit within the box of the label they have for you, is one good way.

If you are in sales and a potential client for your service is frustrated within three seconds of you calling, you can humanize yourself by saying something like,

"Look, I'm calling to help with this service. If you don't need it, that's cool. All you have to do is say so."

With the right tonality, you'll get an answer like,

"Oh, sorry, I'm just having a rough day. I really don't need the service right now, and I'll keep you in mind if I do."

For a dating example, a way to do it when you get a cold shoulder could be,

"Hey, I get it, I'm probably the fifth person that has approached you tonight, and you have to figure out how to get the next creep to go away because you just want to enjoy your evening without being bothered. I'd love to have a conversation to see if we connect and if you're not in a place for that, no worries. Just say so."

In both examples, there's a good chance you will become a person to them because, to them, you've behaved as a human being with a heart and feelings. Suddenly, rather than being the faceless creep sent to get in the way of a good night, you can be a human to them since you haven't behaved the way the object of 'faceless creep' typically does in their mind. It doesn't guarantee any kind of result; it just opens the possibility of connecting human to human.

How do you shift others from object to person? An exercise is useful here.

- Think about three situations in the past week where you may have treated a person as an object. Write them down if that's helpful. Next, write down a potential backstory to humanize these people.

- Now, write how you would have treated them instead had you been conscious of that backstory while interacting with them.

Example 1

1. I sent an aggressive email to my internet provider.

2. The person who fields my email at the internet provider just lost their mother a couple of weeks ago and has been having a really hard time. They just got screamed at by the third

customer today and are wondering if any nice people are left in the world.

3. I would have addressed the issue with my internet provider calmly and respectfully, insisting that they fix it.

Example 2

1. I yelled at a telemarketer.

2. Sharon rides a train and a bus and then walks twenty minutes both ways to get to a job where people threaten her or yell at her most of the day. She does this with a smile because she knows that this job will help feed her children.

3. I would have politely and firmly let her know that I was not a prospective customer, wished her a good day, and hung up.

Example 3

1. I complained to the drive-thru order-taker when they got my order wrong, telling him it couldn't be that hard to get a simple drive-thru order right.

2. Chris, a high school student, works three jobs to pay his mom's mortgage because she got laid off. As the oldest of 4 with a single mom, originally from a country where they spoke a different language, he had to give up his dreams of the NBA and quit the basketball team, where he was the best player, so that his mom could stay in the house that she worked hard for 20 years to be able to buy. On top of that, it is his first day at this job, and he's taking orders in his second language.

3. I would have acknowledged that I might not have spoken clearly enough in my order or that he might have been distracted by another customer and simply asked him to correct the order at the window.

Your turn. Original story, then a new backstory, then what you might have done instead.

_____

_____

This isn't about blame or guilt. At times, we all treat others as objects. It is about awareness of when we do this, how it negatively affects our life experience and working to change it. Living in a world full of objects creates suffering and separation from life.

The more we see and treat others in our world as mere background objects, the colder and lonelier the world can feel. This behavior disconnects us from our humanity.

The good news is, if we don't want to be objectified based on our roles, we can do something to change this. We can take control by ensuring that we humanize those we interact with. By doing this, it will rub off on others. Regardless of whether we continue to be objectified by others, our experience of life will be richer for living in a world of humans rather than 'objects'.

Your ability to be curious about others, humanize and understand them will create deeper connections. Being able to create deeper connections will help you get more of what you want in life in a way that doesn't take from others. Secondarily, these habits will also create more money and success for you.

Neuro-Linguistic Programming, or NLP for short, which could be defined as the study of communication, teaches the belief that "Everyone is doing the best they can with the resources they have." Seeing others as people instead of objects is a byproduct of this belief. If you see your world through this lens, you will have a deeper and more fulfilling experience of life.

The shift from person to object or object to person may be subtle, yet the effect is incredible. In any interaction, the best results will always come when you are treated as a person, not an object, and you are able to humanize anyone you may have inadvertently 'objectified' in the past.

User Error

Have you ever gotten the 'user error' message while working with a computer? Then, after getting the error message, have you ever assaulted your computer with profanity and mashed on your keyboard? This of-

Why is it human nature for us to think there is something wrong with reality based on our perception of it?

ten happens with reality, too. Instead of slowing down to assess the 'user error,' we think the problem exists outside of us. Why is it human nature for us to think there is something wrong with reality based on our perception of it?

The challenge with believing the problem is outside of you is that it also makes you believe the solution is outside of you. That tends to disempower you. External reality isn't your problem. You are. Fortunately, you are also your solution.

People typically put 100 times more effort into changing their external reality than changing their perception of it. If you're waiting for the external world to change, you've given your control away to external factors, which feels so natural to do. What an odd tendency, though! It's like misspelling a word and blaming the pen. It's like driving a car on flat tires and saying the road needs work. It's like looking in the mirror and blaming the shirt company for printing the words on the shirt backward or staring into the sun and screaming at it to stop shining in your eyes.

> *The challenge with believing the problem is outside of you is that it also makes you believe the solution is outside of you.*

Are you wondering if you've given away any of your empowerment to external forces? If any of your thoughts begin with "if (external thing happens), then I'll get (the thing I want/need)," then you have given away your ability to empower yourself. In those areas, your control is gone unless the "if" is something directly in your control. Yet, we can get it back!

Adjusting your perception has a profound effect on your world. Mahatma Gandhi said, "If you want to change the world, start with yourself," and the best place to start is with what you have the most control over, your perception.

This adjustment is the most important ingredient in empowerment. Changes in your perception will absolutely change your world. Otherwise, you'll be forever waiting on the world to change. The musician, John Mayer, captures this perspective best in his song of the same name, "We just feel like we don't have the means to rise above and beat it, so we keep waiting, waiting, waiting on the world to change." If understanding and utilizing our perception is the key to empowerment, we must first look at the ways in which our perception is influenced.

You are now and have been your entire life, looking through glasses at the outside world. They have different colored lenses that seemingly change on their own. Some show the world in a grey tint, some bring out the vibrance of your environment, and some turn everything a dark red.

If your glasses get smudged, you might say the world is blurry. This would be correct from your perspective, yet other people looking through clean glasses would disagree, and they would be correct from their perspective, too. Telling them they are an idiot for believing that the world isn't blurry would be crazy, yet that's exactly what we do. The mistake comes from looking through our glasses at the world and believing that because we see the world that way, that's the way the world is.

The mistake comes from looking through our glasses at the world and believing that because we see the world that way, that's the way the world is.

Now, if I switch out your glasses for another pair that magnifies everything, your perception changes. You might wonder why everyone is always up in your business. If I give you a lens that makes everything seem skinny, like the fun-house at the fair, that's how you'll believe things are.

It is as if a practical joke has been played on everyone. Many different lenses have been added to your glasses that you weren't aware of. A lot of them came from early childhood, and plenty have been added since then.

Some of you may have realized that you were wearing these glasses at a younger age and started to examine them, wondering how they got on your face and who put them there.

Some of you may realize as you read this that someone put them on you without your knowledge.

Some of you may feel like they were superglued to your face and you can't get them off.

Some of you might fear what happens if you take them off. Will it blind me? Will my eyeballs fall out of my head? What if I can't see?

Perhaps you don't feel you are wearing glasses and believe you see everything exactly as it is. If this is the case, just go with me on this.

As you start to act on the courage that has been lying dormant within you, you'll notice that as you take the glasses off, examine them, and adjust them, you'll begin to see more clearly than you ever have before.

As you look at your glasses and notice things about them, don't waste energy on blame or judgment. If your parents put them on you, just take them off now that you know you're wearing them. Self-judgment won't change anything. Celebrate instead now that you know you are not your glasses. They are just glasses. Since they are yours and yours alone, you'll notice that you can add, remove, or change any lenses on them. What a powerful feeling that is! So, as you take them off, easily and effortlessly, hold them up to the light, and let's take a closer look at them.

Your unconscious mind has been influenced by your environment, which is partly responsible for your beliefs and values. These influence your thoughts and attitudes, what you focus on, and the meaning you assign to everything. These beliefs, values, attitudes, and thoughts affect the emotions you experience, which play a large role in the actions you do or do not take.

As we look at each of these variables, keep in mind that each of them interacts with the others and affects the system as a whole. This system, your glasses, is what we are labeling your 'perception.' It means that the more aware you are of the influences of these variables, the more control you have and the more you can empower yourself.

Still confused? That's okay; it will make more and more sense as we get deeper into the book.

Environment

I grew up on a hundred acres in a town without a population sign, fifteen minutes outside of a town of 12,000 people where I went to school. The main store for groceries and necessities was thirty minutes from our home —pre-Amazon days, where ordering online meant waiting two weeks. The closest mall was two and a half hours away.

Today, I can have anything I want delivered to my door in two days or drive three minutes and get it myself. You would think that would stop me from fretting when I realize that the batteries in the remote are dead. It doesn't. Every time it happens, I flash back to my eight-year-old self, knowing that I'll have to switch the one set of batteries I have left between the four remotes that need them and stressing that the lifeline to control my devices might go out completely. My childhood environment taught me that anything that ran out was going to take two weeks of waiting or begging my parents to drive an hour round-trip for the item. Yes, at this point, I could use what I've learned to change that belief. I don't, though, because it stands as a reminder for me of just how powerful our early environments are. This reminder helps me continue to examine how my environment has influenced me and prompts me to search for any limitations I may be putting on my life based on what I learned at an early age.

If the difficulty of replacing batteries and the stress from those incidents have stayed with me for decades, what else has hung around?

What about you? What is your childhood self still holding onto that is limiting you?

Of course, a fear of batteries running out doesn't compare to the physically or emotionally abusive childhood situations many have experienced. Being emotionally abused as a child or growing up in extreme poverty obviously influences your beliefs, emotions, and values. What about those that had a great childhood by any normal standard? Even in the most supportive environments, beliefs get inadvertently adopted. Unhealthy emotional patterns can develop. Sometimes, the 'I had a great childhood' belief can keep us from digging deep enough into the earliest influences on our programming. Now we've put something else in the 'above examination' box.

By no means am I saying that you didn't have a great childhood. Parents are human. If you are a parent, I'm sure you agree with that. Parents have only so much control over the development of their child's beliefs and emotions. Beliefs are also picked up from other sources in the environment. The TV show, the friend at school, the other kids on the bus, the babysitter, and the neighbor. Even though your childhood might have been amazing, there is still a vast amount of insight to be gained from reflecting on it. Sometimes, the message sent is different from the message received. Remember, we can't work with it if we aren't aware of it.

Let's raise our awareness with an exercise. Write your answers to as many of these as possible. This list isn't comprehensive, so go as far as you'd like with it.

- What was your environment like when you were very young?

- What positive and negative associations did you make based on that environment?

- Was there stability in your household?

- How did you need to behave to be safe or to receive love?

- What did you need to do to get attention from your parents?

- How did you have to act to get what you wanted?

- What behaviors were rewarded? What behaviors were punished?

- Did you receive more attention for things you did well or things you didn't do well?

- How was expressing emotion modeled for you?

- Were you allowed to have problems as a child?

- How were you responded to when you expressed emotions?

- If you had siblings, what was your role (caretaker, the baby of the family, etc.)?

- What was your role with your parents (always needed their help, allowed to be a carefree child, needed to fix everything so they wouldn't get upset)?

What other environments were you in as a child? Potential examples include grandparents' homes, after school programs, churches, summer camps, school buses, friends' houses, vacations, babysitters, and parents' offices. Each environment influences us, so answer some of the same questions above within these other environments. We're simply looking for patterns. It may be the meaning you've equated to certain actions or circumstances, behavioral patterns you learned to run to get a certain reward or avoid a certain punishment, or beliefs you've adopted.

Write anything and everything that comes to mind below. Looking back through your answers, which of those do you feel are at the root of limiting beliefs that you have adopted? Take these answers and save them for some of the exercises later in the book. Even if you aren't sure what to do with what you've uncovered yet, celebrate that you have taken the first step toward empowering yourself by consciously identifying them.

_____

_____

_____

The Shadow

Theorized by Jung as existing within the Unconscious Mind, the Shadow is said to be things that are considered unacceptable by society or by an individual. Thus we choose not to acknowledge them as part of us. Put more technically: The Shadow is part of the personality

The Shadow is part of the personality within the unconscious that the ego does not identify in itself.

within the unconscious that the ego does not identify in itself. It consists of what we believe is 'not us'. The Shadow comprises all the aspects of ourselves that we do not wish to recognize and have put into the 'not me' category. Here are a couple of examples.

- I am not an angry person.

- I would never hurt someone else.

- I am never dishonest.

This next part is a little tricky since our unconscious mind is always working to help us move toward increasing wholeness. Much like the sun creates visible shadows when it shines on us and allows us to see the outline of ourselves where light is absent, our Shadow projects unresolved 'Shadow issues' out onto our world for resolution. We will do an exercise that will help this make more sense.

In the first lines below, write the things that are 'not you'. Example: "I am never dishonest."

_____

_____

Now, write out something negative that you consistently experience. It may be that everyone in your world is dishonest with you. Maybe they are constantly pushy. Maybe a lot of people in your world are selfish. Write these out. For example: "Others consistently lie to me or deceive me."

_____

_____

Now take everything you wrote down and do some soul-searching. Assume for a moment that your unconscious mind is hiding from you the ways in which you are the way you said you aren't or that you are guilty of what you believe everyone else is doing.

Here are several examples first:

- I am not an angry person —> I get angry with myself often. Or, I have a deep sense of rage that comes to the surface at times, and I'm just now realizing it.

- I would never hurt someone else—> I hurt people all the time by shutting them out or emotionally freezing them out. Or, I have the urge to harm someone physically when they cut me off in traffic.

- I am never dishonest —> I lie to myself about who I truly am and who I want to be. Or, I have intentionally lied for the sport of it in situations where no one else could find out the truth.

- People are constantly pushy —> I don't know how to ask for what I want. Or, I dream of forcing others to listen to me or do things the way I tell them.

- People are so selfish —> I am always focused negatively on myself, what I've done wrong, and whether my needs are being met. I realize that if I could get ahead or give someone a hand forward, I'd choose to get ahead.

Now write out the examples in the form of 'I' statements.

_____

_____

_____

Would you ever kill someone? Our instinctive reaction to the question of whether we would ever kill someone is, of course, no.

And yet, if you were in a situation where there was a gun in your hand in a room with another person and only one of you could walk out, who would you shoot?

What if the other person was terminally ill?

What if by choosing for the other person to live, it would also mean that everyone in your family would die?

What if the other person had just killed the person you love most in the world?

What if by killing this one other person, you would somehow save the entire human race, and if you didn't, everyone else on the planet would die?

Yes, this does sound like some extreme version of The Hunger Games. Yet, can you see how something you may have previously thought was outside your identity is now a possibility with the right circumstances?

We are discussing the Shadow to bring to the surface parts of your perception that, by becoming aware of, can be used to empower yourself. Since the Shadow's nature is a part of the unconscious that the ego does not identify with, bringing it into conscious awareness in an accepting way can start the process of integration. By integrating Shadow issues, the way you perceive those 'selfish, dishonest, angry others', or whatever you might be projecting, will shift, improving your experience of life.[1]

---

1   *There are resources that go much deeper into this. For a deep dive into The Shadow, read Dr. Matt James' Book: Integrate the Shadow: Master Your Path*

Chapter 5

The Unconscious Mind

We've talked a little about the unconscious mind, and I want to expand on what I mean by 'unconscious mind' before we go further into the exercises. Our unconscious mind has a high level of control over our beliefs, values, attitudes, thoughts, and emotions. As we work with these, we are essentially working with our relationship with our unconscious mind.

You wouldn't ignore the existence of someone for twenty, forty, or sixty years and expect to have a solid relationship with them or expect them to listen to you the moment you started ordering them around, right? We need to treat our unconscious mind in the same way.

To gain a better understanding of the unconscious mind's functions and intentions, let's look at some of the prime directives of the unconscious mind from an NLP perspective.[2]

Be forewarned, this chapter, while full of incredible information, is also very dense. Feel free to skip to the next chapter and digest these prime directives at a different pace, such as one per day for a few weeks. One or more of them will blow your mind, but which ones are different for each reader.

---

2   *For a deeper understanding of the prime directives and specifically how they tie into release and integration work, check out Dr. Matt James' book, Mental and Emotional Release®.*

- The unconscious mind stores memories.

The unconscious mind stores memories both temporally (in relation to time) and atemporally (not in relation to time, often in groupings of similar emotions or patterns). Since memories are often tied with the source of a limiting belief or emotion, working with the unconscious mind in belief changes and releasing emotions is vital. Memories are also stored through our perceptual filters, which is why your memory of a family vacation probably differs from your sibling's.

Our memories shape us and leave clues for how best to work with the unconscious, so it is important to know where they are stored for us to work with them.

- The unconscious mind makes associations and learns quickly.

It is like a pattern machine. The unconscious links together similar things and ideas and quickly catches on, saving us time and precious energy.

This tendency can be great for efficiency. It can also fuel assumptive leaps that aren't helpful. If you have several experiences of dating where the person you are dating acts selfishly, the unconscious mind can quickly make the leap to connect those you date to being selfish. This is where beliefs like "everyone I date is selfish" can form and impact your dating outcomes.

- The unconscious mind organizes all of your memories.

The unconscious mind stores all of your memories in a timeline. This organization is part of the basis of Mental and Emotional Release®, a technique that works with beliefs and emotions. Stop for a second and physically point to the direction of your past. Is it behind you, to your left or right, or in front of you? Now point to your future. Can you see how that implies a line? For simple purposes, that is your Timeline.

When you experience events based on a common theme or particular emotion, they form a 'gestalt.' A gestalt is a chronological grouping of similar emotions. This grouping means that when you experience anger, that event of anger connects to all the previous experiences of anger that you have had. Imagine the very first time someone ever feels anger. What do they call it? They have no reference for anger, what it is, or what it means. Once they do experience it and are able to label it as anger based on someone else calling it that, they now have something to use as a reference every time they experience this emotion. In that way, all the experiences of anger are tied to the initial experience of the emotion.

In release work, we work with this initial experience of the emotion. Like the roots of a tree, if we release or resolve the initial experience, the rest of the experiences have lost what was holding them in place.

Imagine a line of boats that are all tied up together. At the end of the line is one boat, and that one boat is the only one with an anchor. As long as the anchor is in place, it will hold all of them in place. The first event, the root of that particular emotion, is like the anchor. Once it is released, the rest of the emotional events of that emotion are released.

- The unconscious mind represses memories with unresolved negative emotions and may keep repressed emotions repressed for protection.

When your unconscious doesn't believe you have the tools to deal with the unresolved negative emotions, it will repress them. If your unconscious believes the emotions surfacing is a greater threat to your well-being than the consequences of repressing them, they will be repressed. The unconscious mind may believe bringing up the emotion will cause more harm than good. Your unconscious mind will keep them repressed until it believes you are equipped to resolve the emotions.

Sometimes we consciously think we are ready to resolve something holding us back, yet the unconscious won't bring it forward for resolution. It may be that our communication with our unconscious isn't getting the message across or that we simply aren't ready for resolution. As we grow, learn, and heal, the unconscious mind will eventually realize we now have the resources to resolve the negative emotion linked to the memory.

As we discussed earlier in the book, it isn't the intention of our unconscious mind that is negative. It is the expression of that intention. Sometimes we have the tools for resolution and our unconscious doesn't yet know it, which is where our connection with our unconscious mind is vital.

- The unconscious mind presents repressed memories for resolution.

The unconscious mind is in charge of surfacing repressed memories when it believes we are ready to resolve them. When it acknowledges we have the tools to sort through an experience and are ready to do so, it will bring the memories forward. This means that if memories are coming forward, your unconscious has faith and belief in you that you have the tools to resolve them.

When a painful memory or experience surfaces out of no-where, it can be your unconscious mind letting your conscious mind know that you now have the tools and environment needed to gain resolution from the memory. This resolution may be in the form of learning a deeper lesson, applying the perspective you now have to the old event, or healthily integrating the memory into your current life experience.

- The unconscious mind runs the body.

You don't think about each breath you take or consciously focus on your heart to keep beating or digestion to happen. When you get a cut, your body knows what to regrow. The unconscious mind has a blueprint of your body as it is now and your body in perfect health. [3]

With physical health, the unconscious mind plays a huge role. If you do everything right on the physical level yet ignore the power and role of your unconscious mind in relation to health, you are missing a huge opportunity for healing.

- The unconscious mind preserves the body.

The unconscious mind is there to help keep you safe. At times, the threat and the unconscious mind's solution to that threat may seem contradictory at the surface. If you get sick all the time and being sick reinforces that you are safe and loved because it is the only time your significant other or family caters to your every need, then your unconscious mind may keep causing that to happen.

Being catered to and feeling safe and loved while sick is a sec-ondary gain from a negative: you getting sick. You will not be able to let it go until you acknowledge and are ready to release the gain that comes with a problem on both the conscious and unconscious levels. If your unconscious mind can help you get the gain from somewhere else while letting go of the problem, that will facilitate healing. Again, your unconscious mind isn't the enemy here, as it always has pure intentions.

- The unconscious mind is the domain of the emotions.

The unconscious is what holds back or brings forward emotions,

---

3   *For a deeper dive into the role of the unconscious mind in healing the physical body, read "The Divided Mind" by John E. Sarno.*

so it is ultimately in charge of them.

If your conscious and unconscious mind aren't on the same page, inappropriate or unwanted emotions may be showing up for you. These emotions are a compass to guide us to work with the unconscious mind in the healing process.

- The unconscious mind is a highly moral being (the morality you learned through environment and experiences).

Most would agree that your childhood environment influenced you greatly, which includes the morals you modeled during those early years. The unconscious is highly moral, so it will hold on to those learnings and influence you through them.

If you were told constantly to "stop asking questions, it's rude," or "we never talk about money," that will be problematic later on. If your profession requires asking questions, as most do, you will experience emotional resistance in the form of fear or guilt every time you ask a question. The same thing could happen if you became a financial advisor and started asking prospects or clients about their financial situation.

When these situations occur, they can be frustrating. It is important to remember that your unconscious mind is on your side and that you can change the beliefs or early morals that you had previously adopted. If you only change them consciously and ignore the unconscious, your success with the change will be short-lived. It is said in NLP that the conscious mind is the goal-setter, and the unconscious mind is the goal-getter. This means that any time you let your guard down, that old programming from earlier in life will slide back into the driver's seat and take control, sabotaging your progress. Once you are able to change that old programming and get your unconscious mind creating momentum with you, you'll have the foundation for long-term success.

- The unconscious mind enjoys serving and needs clear orders to follow.

Your unconscious mind wants to serve you. If your conscious mind is the goal-setter, and your unconscious mind is the goal-getter, then you need to have a greater relationship and communication with your unconscious mind if you want to have more success in your endeavors. Your unconscious mind is very literal. Imagining it as a young child is the best way to think about it. You must be clear and direct to get your point across when communicating with a child.

For example, if you tell a 5-year-old that you want more money, they'll search all over the house, in the couches, in the drawers, and bring you back thirty-seven cents. You have a very proud child thinking they've accomplished the mission because you now have more money. If you get angry and yell at them because what you actually wanted was a million dollars, how are they going to feel? Is the 5-year-old child to blame? Of course not, because they did exactly what you asked. You just needed to be more specific. It is the same with your unconscious mind. You must be clear and precise about your desired result when you set goals and intentions.

You must be clear and precise about your desired result when you set goals and intentions.

- The unconscious mind controls and maintains all perceptions.

The unconscious mind takes in millions of bits of information each second, while the conscious mind can only take in hundreds. We only consciously receive a tiny fraction of the information our unconscious mind processes. If we consciously took in all of the information all of the time, it would overload us, and we would lose our minds.

So, what's in charge of filtering the 99.99% and giving the remaining fraction to the conscious mind? Yes, it is the unconscious mind. The unconscious mind controls the values, beliefs, and other programming that make up our perception, which filters down to the information we consciously receive.

This is why it's problematic if we are attempting to solve perception challenges only through the conscious mind. We must also work with the unconscious mind when resolving limiting beliefs and emotions.

The unconscious mind controls the values, beliefs, and other programming that make up our perception, which filters down to the information we consciously receive. This is why it's problematic if we are attempting to solve perception challenges only through the conscious mind.

- The unconscious mind generates, stores, distributes and transmits energy.

The unconscious mind is in charge of our energy. Low energy, inappropriate fight-or-flight responses, or too much energy typically come from the unconscious mind.

When working with the unconscious mind in relation to energy, we can uncover the circumstances that caused the unconscious mind to withhold energy or find and release emotional baggage that is siphoning this energy. Emotional baggage can be like climbing a hill with an extra 50-pound rucksack. The moment you drop the rucksack, you gain access to more of your energy by releasing the very thing that was taking so much of it.

- The unconscious mind maintains instincts and generates habits.

Since the unconscious mind can handle so much more bandwidth than the conscious mind, it constantly finds ways to take over processes. Without this, you wouldn't be able to drive a car while thinking about other things or talk to someone while walking. We take this process for granted because, for most people, the majority of our day is now habitual. However, the unconscious doesn't differentiate between good and bad habits. It can get stuck making something more efficient that we really don't want to become a habit. If we want to get in better physical shape through early morning exercise, and our unconscious has developed the habit of hitting the snooze button forty-seven times, that's obviously a problem.

The unconscious mind also maintains our instincts. None of us would be here right now if our ancient ancestors didn't have a sensitive unconscious awareness of potential threats. Sometimes these instincts or habits can become problematic in pursuing what we consciously want to do. If we want to master speaking in front of large crowds, yet our unconscious mind sees a large crowd as a threat, then the well-intentioned instinct can get in the way of what we're consciously wanting.

Remember, our unconscious mind's intention is always to help and support us. When conflicts arise between our unconscious mind and our conscious mind, that conflict is often because we don't have the tools to effectively communicate with our unconscious mind and stay on the same page.

- The unconscious mind needs repetition until the habit is installed.

The more you repeat the action or pattern, the faster it becomes a habit, which works for good and bad habits.

As Warren Buffet has said: "The chains of habit are too light to be felt until they are too heavy to be broken." When we don't want a negative habit to form, we must remain aware of our small daily activities and how often we are doing them. If you grab an alcoholic drink every time you finish your workday, it will quickly become a habit.

For habits you want to be ingrained, you can boost them through visualization, which is a form of imagining outcomes as if they have already happened.

There are many studies that show the unconscious mind learns faster while adding visualization to learning a skill. By imagining yourself doing the action that you want to become a habit, step by step, over and over, you can ingrain it more quickly. If you struggle with getting up with your alarm or starting the new fitness routine you want to start, use visualization to help speed up the process of it becoming a habit.

It's not a question of if you will develop habits. It is a question of whether the habits you develop will help move you toward what you want or away from what you want in your life. Pay close attention to anything that you want to avoid becoming a habit.

- The unconscious mind functions best as a whole, integrated unit (not parts).

If a rowing team has half of the people rowing in one direction and half rowing in the other, they won't go anywhere, no matter how hard they row. If everyone except for one person is rowing in the same direction, this single person will still cause huge problems. They will have inconsistent results at best, and a massive amount of energy will be burned as the rowing team fights against itself.

The unconscious mind is the same. It will perform best when functioning as a whole, integrated unit. If there are parts that have separated off and are rowing against the rest, they will not function well. In NLP, unconscious 'parts' are similar to the rower that has separated and is doing their own thing. The 'part' is a fragment of the unconscious that has separated from the whole and has its own values and beliefs, almost like a separate person. When parts separate in the unconscious mind, they can create inner conflict. We will go more into parts and how to re-integrate in a later chapter.

What's important to know here is that part of our journey is the path of bringing the parts that have split off back into the whole, moving us toward wholeness and healing so that we can be in better alignment with ourselves.

- The unconscious mind is symbolic (uses and responds to symbols).

Communication from the unconscious isn't always straightforward. It can come through as a feeling or a random thought in a quiet moment. It can also come through dreams or sensations in the body. It would be a mistake to take that communication literally. It is often symbolic, so a recurring dream where you are the passenger in a car that wrecks doesn't actually mean you are going to end up in a car wreck.

Being able to create space and receive this communication from the unconscious mind is important. If you don't, your unconscious mind may find more aggressive ways of being heard. The more we listen to our unconscious mind, the more we develop a relationship with this powerful force and are able to live our lives with less inner resistance and more flow.

- The unconscious mind takes everything personally.

To the unconscious mind, everything is about us. What you see in others, your unconscious mind sees within you, and vice versa.

One of the keys to finding things to work on within ourselves is to take note of what we see the most in others, just as we discussed in the section on The Shadow. Is everyone around you constantly angry? Does it feel like everyone is judging you all of the time? Well, it is much more likely that you have a high level of self-judgment that you may or may not be aware of and you are projecting that onto others. This awareness can be a great way to guide us to places within ourselves that can benefit from healing.

- The unconscious mind works on the principle of least effort (path of least resistance).

The unconscious mind will put in the least effort possible to achieve the desired result, which is great for energy conservation and humanity's long-term survival.

Think of this like making wishes to the Genie. In the remake of Aladdin, when his first wish is to become a prince, Genie says,

"There's a lot of gray area in 'make me a prince'" and shows him an alternative version of his wish that would technically be the fulfillment of his wish. He then gives a piece of wisdom for how we can work with our unconscious mind, "Be specific with your words; the deal is in the detail."

- The unconscious mind does not process negatives.

If I say, "don't think of a purple elephant", what does your mind automatically show you? You have to first think of a purple elephant in order to think of anything other than a purple elephant.

We often send confusing messages to the unconscious mind. If we go through life always thinking about what we don't want, you can imagine what the unconscious will bring you more of. If we constantly say or think things like "I don't want to get sick, I don't want to be overweight, or I don't want to be single anymore," then we are directing the unconscious mind to focus on sickness, being overweight, and being single.

When learning to golf, I would get to the tee box on a hole where I had to hit it over the water. I often made the mistake of telling myself over and over, "don't hit it into the water," and then I would hit it directly into the pond. It took a while to realize that I had to first think about hitting it in the water to follow that thought. I wasn't focused at all on where I did want to hit the ball.

What if you are giving a speech or performing something, and you tell yourself over and over, "don't mess up?" You are focusing on messing up.

I can't overstate the importance of this in setting goals. If the goal is not to be financially broke, we will most likely reach a point where we aren't broke and then slide back into being broke and continue that cycle. We are going away from being broke, and we have to keep focusing on being broke to assess if we are progressing away from it accurately. A better goal would be to create a certain amount of wealth, with an ongoing focus on becoming wealthier and wealthier every day. To effectively set goals that the unconscious will support, we must state them in the positive and be clear on the outcome we desire.

To effectively set goals that the unconscious will support, we must state them in the positive and be clear on the outcome we desire.

Chapter 6

Our Relationship with Our Unconscious Mind

War

It is medieval times. You are at war. You've been at war for as long as you can remember. It feels like it's all you've ever known. Fear and anger, aggression and defense. You are afraid and tired. You are hiding in the cave, and you hear the dragon roar. You have the choice to retreat, to hide in the cave indefinitely. You can stay in the dark and damp where it's safe, but you don't love the idea, even though the cave is familiar. You've spent so much time here that you know every wall and stone, and you know it well.

You have the choice. The existential consequences of this decision paralyze you.

Somehow, something in you makes the decision you didn't know you were capable of. You step toward the light, and toward the dragon, toward an uncertain fate. You hear the sound of scales sliding against stone as you inch closer. You see the sky's reflection in the lake that touches the cave's entrance. It's so bright outside that you close your eyes as you emerge, feeling the sun hit your face. Terrified, you hear the deafening sound of wings as you are lifted off the ground. Too afraid to open your eyes, you silently lament. This must be the end. Higher and higher you go.

Suddenly, you feel yourself falling, and your eyes jerk open.

You see the dragon snarling as it speeds toward you. You open your arms wide in surrender, and something unbelievable happens. The dragon stops, wings spread wide. You both blink, and you start to realize. You realize something that you'd forgotten. The dragon you see as you float there… is you. You are looking at your own reflection in the lake. 'The dragon' isn't who you were at war with. You were at war with yourself. At that moment, everything changes.

"And as you read, you may begin to notice…

that the one who was fighting the dragon…

and the one who seemed to be the dragon…

may not be as separate as they once appeared.

And as you notice that…

it can become possible to allow your mind to soften a little…

to let both be true at once.

And in allowing both…

and neither…

to be who you are…

you may begin to experience something quieter…

The simple noticing of yourself.

And if you are noticing yourself…

you might become curious…

about who is not doing the noticing."

You are beginning to realize that your unconscious mind is always your ally. If you feel at odds with your unconscious mind, it is because you are not communicating effectively with it. This isn't a fault or blame statement. It is one to give you hope and excitement and help you know where to focus. As you improve your communication with your unconscious mind, you'll be able to get more of what you want out of life. You can stop feeling like you are swimming upstream and create more purposeful progress toward your goals and dreams.

Our unconscious mind is amazing and extremely powerful. Depending on how we perceive it, it can be one of our greatest allies or greatest enemies. Understanding the relationship between our unconscious and conscious mind is imperative to move toward empowerment. Have you ever wanted something consciously, and it felt like something was resisting you deep down? Have you found yourself reacting to situations in ways that make no sense to you? In those times, your conscious and your unconscious mind aren't on the same page. The natural reaction might be to get frustrated with your unconscious mind, judge it, blame it, or blame yourself for being unable to fix it. All of those would be a waste of energy. Plus, it's hard to have great communication with someone if you see them as the enemy.

It is always the approach of the unconscious mind, never the intention, that causes the challenges. This is so important. The goal is effective communication with your unconscious; the first step to that is understanding you are on the same team. The intention of your unconscious mind is pure. It is there to support you. The unconscious mind is like a young child. Pure intentions, putting out maximum effort, yet it can sometimes misunderstand our communication with it. If you veer off the road and drive into a tree, is your car at fault? Of course not. And don't even consider going down a shame spiral thinking the problems you have must be your fault on a conscious level. That would also be incorrect. Most of our challenges on the unconscious level can be labeled as a miscommunication. This miscommunication can create suffering. Communication between the two is the foundation of alignment and healing. Sometimes, the unconscious does exactly what we need at the time and what it believes will protect us. It was as if the button got stuck, and the unconscious continued doing it. It kept going because that's what it thought would serve you, and now you've lost the controls, so you can't communicate that you don't need that behavior anymore.

Let's imagine you are in a cage. Is that a good thing or a bad thing? It depends. If you are in a cage in your crazy neighbor's basement, you'd want to escape it as quickly as possible. If you

It is always the approach of the unconscious mind, never the intention, that causes the challenges.

are in a shark cage, the last thing you'd want to do is get out of it. Sometimes your unconscious mind thinks you are in a shark cage, and your conscious mind thinks you are in your neighbor's basement, or vice-versa.

This misunderstanding is where the challenge comes in. You are fighting like mad to get out of the cage while your unconscious is doing its best to keep you in the cage. You both have the same intention: your safety. The expression of that intention results in polar opposite action. If we simply look at the expression of the intention, it appears that our unconscious and conscious minds are in conflict. If we can realize that the intentions are the same, it creates the basis for more effective communication between the conscious and unconscious. This creates healing, synergy, and a greater level of empowerment.

A Better Expression

Let's look at an example. Chris grew up in a home where if he spoke out of turn, his father would slap him or call him stupid. Chris's unconscious mind quickly learned that staying quiet was what protected him. As his childhood continued, he got into situations where teachers would call on him in school. It felt like a big threat to Chris because why would it be any different than when he spoke up at home?

In further service to protect him, his unconscious also took on the belief that he is stupid because believing that kept him out of situations his unconscious believed were a threat. He went on to college, barely getting accepted because he had unconsciously made his grades reflect this belief of being stupid. He had a girlfriend at the time, and she noticed that Chris was exceptionally gifted in understanding others. He was often quiet, yet when he did talk to her about what he saw with other students or teachers, she was amazed. She encouraged him to pursue a path where he could use this ability, and he ended up graduating and becoming a skilled therapist.

Throughout a decade of successful therapy practice, he was asked to lead a group of therapists, speak on several occasions, and encouraged to write a book. He turned all of it down. His girlfriend, who had become his wife, confronted him about it. She said, "There are many people who could be positively impacted by what you know. Why have you turned down all the opportunities to do so?"

He had no idea. All he knew was that he would become afraid any time opportunities came up. He'd start sweating and feel like running out of the room, yet he wanted so badly to help others. That is why he chose to be a therapist. What he hadn't realized is that his unconscious mind was attempting to protect him by holding onto the belief that he was stupid and that staying quiet would protect him. The fear, sweating, and wanting to run out of the room was his unconscious mind doing everything it could to protect him. His unconscious mind was attempting to protect him from what it saw as crazy and dangerous behavior while he was attempting to push through what he believed was an irrational response that showed up every time he thought about speaking, leading a group, or writing a book.

This situation is an example of the miscommunication that can happen with the unconscious mind when we act in ways that it thinks are threatening our safety. The unconscious mind needs new information and direction. What was very useful in protecting Chris when he was young became the biggest obstacle to what he wanted to accomplish next.

Chris's story is not an uncommon one. In western culture, the connection between the unconscious mind and the conscious mind, and even the existence and role of the unconscious mind, has been misunderstood for a very long time. We often think we must simply 'push through' when beliefs or emotions surface that we feel are holding us back. This automatically creates inner conflict. By thinking we should 'push through,' we are identifying our own beliefs as obstacles, as the enemy.

How much of our precious energy does it take to fight against our own unconscious mind? The unconscious mind never stops, never sleeps, and never tires. Who in the world would purposefully choose to fight that opponent every day?

The Escalator

Imagine life as an endless escalator that we are climbing, with growth, success, and the things we want as points along the escalator. When we choose to fight against our unconscious mind, it is like choosing to go the wrong way up an escalator. You can make progress while running, except you eventually have to take a break. At some point, you need to sleep. When you stop moving, you are slowly carried back down the escalator. You go to sleep and wake up, realizing that you are almost back at the bottom. You grit your teeth and run even harder and faster. Satisfied at the end of the day, you stop and sleep. You wake up horrified to find that you are nearly back to where you started again. It must be an effort issue, you decide. You aren't pushing hard enough. You drag yourself up, tired and sore, start running and do it all over again. Each day, you wake up to find that most of the previous day's progress has been lost to that soul-sucking escalator. It seems akin to the story in Greek Mythology of Sisyphus. In it, Sisyphus is condemned to roll a boulder up to the top of a hill, only to have the rock roll back down to the bottom every time he gets close to the top.

Since you know escalators can go both ways, what if you can find a way to reprogram the escalator to go up? You figure out how to reprogram it to change directions. Now, you wake up and run up the escalator until you are tired, like usual. This time, though, as you rest on the escalator, you realize you are still moving forward. You finish for the day and go to sleep. When you wake, you realize you are farther along than when you went to sleep. How would that affect how far you are able to get? How would that impact what you can accomplish? How would you feel if that was your experience every day?

It's time for you to start working with your escalator. It's time for you to understand its mechanics, understand how to change its programming, and figure out what causes it to move in the direction it is moving. As you do, you'll learn how to get your escalator to work in alignment with what you want.

Now, it's time for an exercise. Stay with me and keep playing all in. Understanding the concepts is part of it. Engaging with them is the other part.

Look for the places where you feel the most drag against what you are striving to accomplish. Where does it feel like your conscious and unconscious mind are working in opposition? I've included examples below to point you in the right direction.

Use the lines to describe the situations or common occurrences in your life where you feel unconscious resistance. Leave space after each for the next part of the exercise.

Example:

• When my child gets upset with me, the voice in my head screams that I'm a terrible parent and am not good enough.

• In our company meetings, I have so much to share and want to share, yet I get a huge lump in my throat every time I think about speaking up.

• Every time I try to sit down and budget, I get this horrible feeling of being a failure and can't do it.

• <u>When I start writing out goals for my business, I start thinking that "I'm not smart enough" and "who am I?" to set such high goals.</u>

_____

_____

_____

_____

As we discussed earlier, when there is conflict, it is the expression of the intention that is in conflict between your conscious and unconscious mind, not the intention itself. The unconscious mind always has a positive intention.

Now, go back to what you wrote and write next to them both the intention for your conscious and your unconscious mind.

Example:

• <u>When my child gets upset with me, the voice in my head screams that I'm a terrible parent and am not good enough.</u>

» Conscious: I want to raise a healthy and respectful child.

» Unconscious: Feeling guilt and shame ensures I'll work harder at parenting.

» Conscious: I want life success for my child.

» Unconscious: If I feel bad about myself, I'll be a better parent.

• <u>In our company meetings, I have so much to share and want to share, yet I get a huge lump in my throat every time I think about actually speaking up.</u>

» Conscious: I want to contribute by speaking up.

» Unconscious: If I speak up, people will realize I'm not good enough to work here.

» Conscious: I want to contribute.

>> Unconscious: I want to avoid being seen as not good enough.

- <u>Every time I try to sit down and budget, I get this horrible feeling of being a failure and can't do it.</u>

  >> Conscious: I want to budget to create financial progress and freedom.

  >> Unconscious: I don't want to be a failure, so I avoid budgeting because it makes me feel like a failure.

  >> Conscious: I want financial progress and freedom.

  >> Unconscious: I don't want to be a failure.

- <u>When I start writing out goals for my life, I start thinking that "I'm not smart enough" and "who am I?" to set such big goals.</u>

  >> Conscious: I want to have clear goals for my life.

  >> Unconscious: I don't like to write goals because it makes me feel not smart enough and inadequate.

  >> Conscious: I want progress and success.

  >> Unconscious: I don't want to feel not smart enough and inadequate.

As you can see, the intentions are always pure. Now, acknowledge the validity of your unconscious mind's intentions and thank it for doing its best to follow through on those intentions. Let's continue further with these.

Since most of the statements will be action-related, they can be rewritten into a "this action means this" or "this action will cause this." Rewrite your statements into that form now.

- <u>Feeling bad about myself as a parent causes me to be a better parent.</u>

- <u>Speaking up will reveal that I'm not good enough.</u>

- <u>Doing a budget will cause me to feel like a failure.</u>

- <u>Writing out business goals will prove I'm inadequate and not smart enough.</u>

_____

_____

_____

_____

_____

_____

Now, pull the limiting belief from each statement and write it below.

- <u>I'm a bad parent.</u>

- <u>I'm not good enough.</u>

- <u>I feel like a failure.</u>

- <u>I'm inadequate and not smart enough.</u>

_____

_____

_____

_____

_____

_____

Run each statement, one at a time, through these 2 sets of questions:

[Being a bad parent]

1. What is it?

2. What is it not?

3. How do you know what it is not?

4, What do you need to not know to know this?

1. What would happen if you were [inadequate]?

2. What wouldn't happen if you were [inadequate]?

3. What would happen if you weren't [inadequate]?

4. What wouldn't happen if you weren't [inadequate]?

Now, go back and rewrite each statement in a positive way.

- Believing I'm a great parent will allow me to help my child the most.

- Speaking up will allow me to contribute to others.

- Doing a budget will help create long-term financial success.

- Writing out life goals will lead to more success and happiness.

_____

_____

_____

_____

_____

_____

_____

_____

_____

_____

_____

These exercises are designed to identify the meaning your unconscious mind is giving to the situation or action, change it, and
help your unconscious see it in a way that allows your conscious
and unconscious mind to be on the same page. If this is still a
bit tricky to understand, that's okay. It will make more and more
sense as we continue on.

Part 2

Elements of your Perception

PTFAR

There is an acronym (originally attributed to T. Harv Eker) that I first encountered in the BOLD program by Dianna Kokoszka. It is PTFAR and stands for Programming, Thoughts, Feelings, Actions, and Results. Illustrated, it looks like this:

This illustration shows that your programming creates your

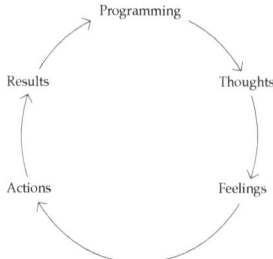

thoughts, which create your feelings, which determine your actions, and results. If you aren't getting the results you desire in life, you can work backward to actions, feelings, thoughts, and beliefs to find what is getting in your way. The obstacle to getting the desired result is often somewhere in the preceding areas in this illustration. If your feeling is the problem, you can look at your thoughts and programming to find and remove the obstacle. Throughout this book, we have already been working with your beliefs, thoughts, and emotions. Now, let's go deeper in.

The exercise in the next chapter is one of my favorites. We have been building toward it. We have already started to pull out your beliefs, thoughts, and emotions and work with them. Now I'd like to suggest a specific belief change.

I want you to focus specifically on one belief—one single belief you can capture in four words—a belief that, by changing just one word, can have a transformative effect on your entire life.

Life Happens <u>To</u> You.

Life Happens <u>For</u> You.

I cannot overstate the power of this change in your empowerment. I'm particularly excited about this one exercise, and it will be worth every minute of the time and energy you invest into it. Play all in.

Chapter 7

Beliefs

From the exercises we've done so far, we have brought to the surface several limiting beliefs. Here is a list of others that you might recognize within yourself.

Potential limiting beliefs:

- I'm an imposter.

- The world is not a safe place. I can't trust others.

- I'm not good enough.

- I'm not good at talking to strangers.

- I'm always tired.

- I'm not a morning person.

- I can't stick to a schedule.

- I'm a slow learner.

- I'll never be fit.

- I'll never be thin.

- I can't be disciplined.

- Following a schedule is impossible for me.

- All _____ are jerks.

- Everyone is always competing with me.

- None of my employees are loyal.

- My hires never stay.

- I'm not negative. I'm just realistic.

- My childhood messed me up, so that's why I am the way I am.

- I could never _____. I am bad.

- I never do anything right. I'm so selfish.

There's a big difference between what is inherently true and what you believe to be true. The good news: beliefs can always be changed.

Beliefs can always be changed.

Believing is Seeing

With perception, believing is seeing more than seeing is believing. When you believe you or the world are a certain way, you will inevitably perceive it that way. Most of us know someone who is in good shape who has told themselves and others they are overweight. If this person holds onto the belief of being overweight, no amount of external reality is going to change that belief. By believing they are overweight, they *When you believe you or the world are a certain way, you will inevitably perceive it that way.* will feel worse and act in ways that support being overweight or aggressively against it in an unhealthy way because those actions fall in line with their belief.

Believing others are untrustworthy is another example of a belief's impact on our perception. With that belief, you'll notice all of the things about them that can be perceived as untrustworthy and ignore anything that could be perceived as trustworthy. If you believe all cold weather is miserable, you'll focus on the misery of how your hands and feet hurt and ignore how crisp and fresh the icy mountain air can be and how still and quiet the world can be when snow covers the ground on a frigid day.

If you hold any of the limiting beliefs from the list of potential limiting beliefs, they will influence how you see your world. You'll see the world through the 'I'm always tired' lens or the 'I'm an imposter' filter.

This is so important to understand. We rarely act in ways that contradict our beliefs about ourselves. Since our beliefs are part of our perception, and our perception determines our actions, we can examine our own behavior to uncover our unconscious beliefs.

Your Relationship With Life

Do you believe that your life is happening to you? Or do you believe your life is happening by you or for you? This is a subtle difference. We're exchanging one word in a single sentence, yet it makes all the difference.

Life Happens <u>To</u> You.

Life Happens <u>For</u> You.

Let's dig deeper into the differences between these ways of experiencing life. As a whole, this is a great way to sum up this book: Helping you go from life happening to you into the other, higher levels of consciousness where life starts to happen for you. Other terms for 'levels of consciousness' could simply be 'wiser' or 'more empowered.' If that works better for you, think of those each time "phases of consciousness" shows up. In the following excerpt, when Mary O'Malley uses the word 'spells', you can also think of it as your beliefs, thoughts, and feelings. I'd like you to read it directly from her. In her book, What's in the Way is the Way, Mary O'Malley explains what she calls "The Six Phases of Consciousness." We will focus on two of them for our purposes. Mary, take it away!

The 1st Level of Higher Consciousness: Life Happens To You

"For a good deal of your life, you have probably lived like most human beings, feeling that Life is happening to you. Life is so big, and if you are honest with yourself, you never really know what is going to happen next. You wake up one morning, and your heart is light and happy, but the next day you're unsettled. Bosses fire you, the flu debilitates you, people you love reject you, every day you get a little older, and death is always lurking around the corner.

It is understandable that the more unconscious you are, the more often you feel like a victim of Life. When you live in the belief that Life is happening to you, you often view Life as a possible threat. So you stay caught in your head, finding yourself lost in your clouds of struggle and listening to a storyteller that resists, reacts, defends, and explains, hoping to figure everything out. It generally does absolutely anything except be open to Life, right here, right now."[4]

The 4th Level of Higher Consciousness: Life Happens For You

"The more you become curious about what is happening rather than reacting and controlling, the more you come to a wonderful realization that your life is for you. Life is not a random series of events. It is a highly intelligent unfolding that is putting you in the exact situations you need in order to see and unhook from the spells that keep you separate from its flow. No matter what is happening in your life, you finally understand that Life knows what it is doing.

Rather than Life being something you have to mold and shape into what you want it to be, you begin to show up for Life exactly

---

4   *"What's in the Way Is the Way"* © *2016 Mary O'Malley, excerpted with permission from the publisher, Sounds True, Inc.*

as it is. Yes, the flow of Life includes pain, loss, and death. But resisting the pains of Life only turn them into suffering, and the suffering that comes from resistance is always much greater than directly experiencing your pain. Instead of tightening around your experiences and turning away from them, which only thickens your clouds of struggle, you bring your attention to your experience, whatever it is.

Even little moments of curiosity sprinkled throughout your day are powerful. Every time you respond rather than react to what is going on inside of you, what was formerly bound up begins to loosen. Remember, your natural state is free-flowing aliveness. When that aliveness gets trapped in the spells, your energy and joy dim. When the spells receive the light of your attentiveness, they let go, and the trapped energy flows freely, bringing with it the bliss of openness. Remember, Life is set up to bring up what has been bound up, so it can open up to be freed up, and you can show up for Life." [5]

Now that you understand these two levels more deeply, it's time for the exercise. Stop and take the time to do this. Even if it feels terribly uncomfortable to sit and do it, you will be grateful you did. Even if you start it and then think of a thousand other things that you 'need to do right now', stay with the exercise. Sometimes in life, you make a choice that seems insignificant at the moment. Only when you look back do you realize it was a truly significant one.

As Steve Jobs put it, "You can't connect the dots looking forward; you can only connect them looking backwards…" This may be one of those moments for you, and there's only one way to know for sure. By doing it, you could gain a sense of clarity about your journey and a tremendous amount of purpose in exchange for minutes of your life. By not doing it, you could gain half an hour that you'd spend on something else, never knowing the cost of missing a moment where you could have made a massive leap forward in the quality of your experience of life. It's always easier at the moment to keep reading and tell yourself you'll come back and do it later, and only you know your track record in following through.

---

5   *"What's in the Way Is the Way"* © *2016 Mary O'Malley, excerpted with permission from the publisher, Sounds True, Inc.*

First, use this page to write the story of your life. Write it in the form of life happening to you. Allow yourself to focus on the tougher experiences you've had. Write them all down in chronological order as best you can. Start from as far back as you can remember. This is the time to get all of it out into the open. Be completely transparent with yourself. Write about the events of hurt and shame. Write about the pain and the heartbreak. Write about your missteps and failures. Do not filter. Allow it all out onto the page. And for this first page I'm going to tell you to do something counterintuitive to the nature of this whole book. Lean into the victim's view of life as you write. Lean into the unfairness of how life has treated you. Fully express any of the blame, frustration, powerlessness, helplessness, hopelessness, unworthiness, and guilt that life has caused. The more you pull that out of yourself and put it on the page as you write your disempowered narrative, the better the foundation will be for your empowered one. Take the time, now, to write it.

_____

_____

_____

_____

_____

_____

_____

_____

_____

_____

_____

_____

_____

Now, write the story of your life again on this page. This time, write everything from the viewpoint of life happening for you. Reference that section from Mary earlier as needed, to hold that perspective. Write about all the things that happened in your life up to this point as if they are the ingredients that have made you who you are and the stepping stones that have prepared you for what's next. Take all of the disempowered narrative you wrote before and reframe it through the lens of all of it being for you, for your empowerment. All of those dark times were preparing you for who you are becoming. All of those hurts came with lessons for you to empower yourself with. They came with insights and tools for how to help yourself and others. You are where you are supposed to be at this moment. All of the pieces have rearranged themselves, just waiting for you to notice them in the right light... to notice them in the reflection of your greatness. Now, write it.

_____

_____

_____

_____

_____

_____

_____

_____

_____

_____

_____

_____

_____

_____

Those experiences have molded you. Notice that some of your greatest accomplishments and growth may have come from experiences that seemed terrible at the time. If you are in the middle of some of those experiences, write about how they are preparing you for something great. From pain, you can gain so much purpose and power if you are able to perceive it in this way. Rise like the phoenix from the ashes of your old story. Choose empowerment. Lean into trusting life on a conscious level. I know you already trust that life is happening for you on some level because your lungs breathe for you, and your heart beats for you. And since you instinctively know how to have this trust, this new story flows naturally from you.

> *Notice that some of your greatest accomplishments and growth may have come from experiences that seemed terrible at the time.*

Stop for a moment and contemplate what you learned about yourself from this exercise. Notice the power of changing the frame we experience life through. None of the facts from your story changed, and yet your entire story changes when viewed through the lens of life happening for you.

If you had a really hard time with this exercise, or skipped it because it was 'not helpful' or because I'm talking like someone who lives in a fairytale land that has never seen true tragedy or disempowering situations, then I'll level with the skeptic in you.

You're right, from an objective reality standpoint, those events weren't inherently good. Nor were they inherently bad. They simply were. Life is. Life flows. We assign the meanings. But you're also wrong, for your own empowerment at least. Because if all objective events in life simply are, in black and white, and we have the choice to color them with our perception, which is the way you'd choose to color them so that you can have the best experience of your life?

All suffering is the resistance to what is. Fearing, blaming, shaming, they're all ways of resisting life as it is.

Life by itself simply is, and is objective. Life as perceived and experienced by a human is always subjective. Choosing and embodying empowerment will always create the best experience of life possible.

I trust that you gained something valuable from taking the time to do this exercise. It is my hope that you have just taken another big step into your empowerment and are realizing just how powerful your perception can be. I trust you are realizing that it is because of our experiences in life, not despite them, that we can find deeper meaning and purpose.

Values

In continuing to explore what our perception is made of, we'll dive into values. Values are also under the umbrella of 'programming' in the PTFAR diagram. Values are one of our deepest levels of programming. They determine what is important to us, motivate us, and direct our behavior. Values determine how we choose to spend our time, and they are the filter through which we evaluate the experiences we have. Knowing our values is an important step in understanding what influences our perception and how to gain more inner alignment.

Values determine how we choose to spend our time, and they are the filter through which we evaluate the experiences we have.

You may have done an exercise working with values before. Most commonly, it is where you take a list of words given to you and sort them into your top values. While this method can point you in the right direction, it has a few challenges. Since values are one of our deepest programming levels, it means they are mostly unconscious, which means it would be hard to pick our actual values out of a list. Also, by giving you a list, the words included are already biasing you. If I say, "What do you value more: family, freedom, or physical fitness?" I am biasing you into selecting from my available choices. Additionally, when picking from a list, you are more likely to end up with values you want to have versus those you actually have. Plus, words have different meanings for each of us. While success may mean something specific to one person, it can often mean something entirely different to another, and your own words or labels are important when working with values.

There are methods based in NLP to elicit values more effectively. 'Eliciting values' is the process of helping someone pull their values from their conscious and unconscious mind. If you want to elicit your values within a certain area of life, an NLP Master Practitioner can help.

For the purposes of this book, I want to help you pull out one value and work through several steps with it, so you can begin to understand the power of our values better. Through a few exercises, you'll get a glimpse of the importance of values in any relationship, including your relationship with yourself. We'll use a romantic relationship in this example, yet it is equally useful in all types of relationships.

Here, I'm asking you about the area of life of intimate relationships, meaning a one-on-one relationship that you could call a significant other, an intimate relationship, marriage, etc. Use whichever label makes sense to you, and I will simply call it 'relationship.'

- What is important to you about [a romantic relationship]?

Let's say you wrote 'trust'. Yay! Now you know one of your values in a relationship. That means all you need to do is share your list of values with your significant other, and then you'll both be on the same page, right?

Not quite. The word trust has different meanings to different people. I'll prove it.

Take the word 'trust' and write five words that equal 'trust' to you. Without showing them your list, ask your partner to write five words synonymous with 'trust'.

Now compare your lists. The likelihood that you had more than 3 of the same words is low.

So, when you say your partner will understand what your value means because they know the word, they are getting a 3-out-of-5, or a 60%, at best. Would you really like them to have the equivalent of the lowest possible passing grade in terms of understanding and meeting your value? Obviously not.

Complex Equivalence (Your Value = Your Definition)

Here is where we start to get clarity. Complex Equivalence is where we are finding out what the word or phrase means to us. It looks like this. (The label) = your meaning.

Now, write out your definition of the word you wrote in the blank above (or said to yourself):

Now we've got it right, almost. Let's say your definition of 'trust' is that your partner never betrays you. Now you take that to your partner, and they should always be able to meet your value of 'trust,' right? Not quite. There's still a gap. We know your value of 'trust' and what it means to you, yet we still don't know exactly how that value is met or violated. We don't know what you consider betrayal, and we don't know how it is that you know that your value of 'trust' is being met. We must continue and clarify both of those.

Next, answer the following:

- What has to happen for your value of [trust] to be violated in a relationship?

- How do you know when your value of [trust] is being met in a relationship?

Now we're getting somewhere. Let's imagine you wrote that your value of trust would be violated if you told something to your partner in confidence and they went and told someone else without your permission. And let's say you answered that you'd feel trust is being met when you can say anything to your partner in confidence, and know that no matter what, they will not judge you. Now there is absolutely no doubt what 'trust' means to you, and you've set your partner up for success regarding 'trust' for you.

How powerful would it be to know your partner's values in a relationship, what they mean to them, and how those values could be met or violated? You would have a guide on their values, how to avoid violating them, and how to meet them in your relationship. Imagine the positive impact this could have on your relationship.

And this isn't only valuable for romantic relationships. Understanding someone's values is the basis of understanding them on a much deeper level and empowers you to have the best relationship possible with that person.

To see how this plays out on a daily basis, let's look at the conversations that can happen in dating and see where our assumptions can cause huge gaps in communication and understanding.

You are in conversation on a dating app or an in-person date, and the question comes up,

"What's important to you in a relationship?"

They say, "trust."

You quickly say, "me too!" and then you move on to other topics.

After what we've discussed, can you see how there might be a big problem in your assumption and that you could find out the hard way that each of you meant something entirely different when you said "trust?"

Let's look at a few common values in relationships and notice how problematic this kind of miscommunication can be.

You are on a first date, and things are going great. When the question comes up, you both say 'trust,' 'quality time,' and 'sex' are important to you in a relationship. Not having clarified what either of you meant by these words, you both leave the date feeling ecstatic. You are so in sync. You have the same important relationship values. You are soulmates and on the same page.

However, what you haven't discussed are your definitions of these values or how they are met or violated. As an example, your definitions and theirs are as follows:

Trust
- Yours: Your partner always keeps your secrets.

- Theirs: You never withhold anything from them, ever.

Quality Time
- Yours: Deep conversations with complete focus on each other.

- Theirs: Spending a lot of side-by-side time together watching movies or listening to music.

Sex
- Yours: Having sex every day and twice on Sundays.

- Theirs: Allowing the sexual tension to build between you for days or weeks until the moment feels most right.

Without knowing these, you work to meet their values based on how you would naturally want them met and avoid violating them in the ways that would violate your values.

You date for a while, and all seems to be going well. Then, you start to notice issues.

- You want to sit with a glass of wine and talk, but your partner keeps turning up the music or wanting to turn on a movie while you are in the middle of a deep discussion.

- Your partner gets upset with you because you didn't tell them about a stressful conversation you had at work last week, saying you violated their trust. You are confused because you haven't ever told anyone what your partner said in confidence. How could you have betrayed their trust?

- On top of all of that, you've shown your interest in sex every day for a week now, and your partner keeps teasing you about it. Resentment starts to build because they told you sex was important, but it clearly seems that they are more interested in teasing you with it.

You are so confused because you have the same top values in a relationship. On the surface, it seems like there wouldn't be any issues, yet both of you are frustrated with the other.

You both want it to work, so you seek out a great counselor. It comes out that trust, quality time, and sex while being top values for both of you, mean completely different things to each of you. By slowing down to learn what they mean to each of you and how to meet those values while avoiding violating them, you start to learn and communicate in each of your unique languages.

You are able to get your relationship back on track based on what you've learned, and now you know how to optimize the quality of the relationship for both of you in a purposeful way. If you've ever had the experience of not knowing what you've done right to have your relationship going so well, or not knowing what you've done wrong when it isn't going well, delving deeper into what your values really are and mean for you can help you find answers.

Not understanding your partner's values or how to fulfill them is like being given a ball and not knowing whether to dribble it, kick it, or hit it with a bat, club, or racket. You pick one that's most natural for you, and sometimes you are rewarded for your choice, and sometimes you are penalized. It's difficult to have success when you don't know the rules or what game you are playing. Do yourself a favor, slow down, and learn the rules.

For those of you thinking this is cheating and that your partner should "just know" your values, think about this: Imagine going to a fancy restaurant with raving reviews. The restaurant is famous for its unbelievable dishes and special process of helping patrons choose a meal based on a thorough process of questions about their likes and dislikes of various foods and spices. You've been told how great it is by at least a dozen people, so you decide you must try it, except you won't be bothered by all the up-front questions. You sit down, and the waiter walks up to you. He asks you what you'd like to eat. You scoff at him and say, "Well, if this is a 5-star restaurant, then you should already know what I want." He looks you up and down, scribbles on a notepad, and disappears.

He returns and proudly serves you a plate with smoked donkey and a side of Jamaican Jerk vegetables.

"Enjoy your 5-star meal," he says.

The meal repulses you. You ask, "What the heck is this?"

"Well, I chose a plate the best I could, but normally we would have gone through our proven process so that we could ensure a high-quality meal and experience," he says.

Do you think you're going to enjoy that meal? Unless you are very adventurous, probably not. You'll also most likely not go back to that restaurant ever again. Would it have been the restaurant's fault? Of course not.

If you're thinking that understanding your partner's values is weird or not that important, here is a different example. You decide it's time to get married to your significant other. You go out, find a jewelry store, and pick out a ring you like. Then, you call that wedding venue that your significant other mentioned looked interesting, and you put down a non-refundable payment on it. After that, you call your cousin Vinny and book his band because heavy metal is surely your partner's favorite type of music, too. Then you book your honeymoon for an ice hotel in Sweden because you both said you wanted to go on a winter vacation someday. You have everything in place. You are at breakfast on a Tuesday at Denny's, and your partner says, "Today is such a nice day; it's so beautiful outside."

You take that as a sign that it's the perfect time and place, and you propose on the spot. Even though you've only been dating a few months and have never discussed marriage, you know they'll say yes because of that look you shared last month and because you know what they meant when they said, "We are really good together."

How do you think that is going to go? If you think it'll go great, please make sure it is on video when you attempt it and send me a copy.

It's an extreme example that seems ridiculous. No sane person would make half of those decisions for a potential spouse, nor would most people want those decisions to be made for them as a potential spouse. Yet, not clarifying your own values or your partner's will lead you to make the same kind of assumptive leaps.

Let's shift to looking at values on a personal level within ourselves. Since values determine what we do with our time and how we evaluate the time we've spent, it follows that when we align our actions properly with our values, it gives us energy and connects us with more meaning in our lives. Let's explore this further.

John is a sales rep in a large company. He has been the top salesperson for two years straight. His sales are double that of the next highest sales rep. The company decides to change up some of its products and focus more on the high-profit margin products in its lineup. They also upgrade their office layout so that each sales rep has their own soundproof private office from where they make their sales calls. Since John has been the top salesperson, they promote him to sales manager, where he sits in his corner office all day listening to live sales calls of the other salespeople. His job now consists of monitoring the other salespeople and cold-calling the biggest potential new clients.

A few months later, things are a mess. John is miserable. Instead of jumping out of bed in the mornings and getting to work early, he is dragging himself in and barely on time. His salespeople are getting mediocre results. Management is confused and questioning their decision to promote him, and he is now contemplating switching careers.

What happened? Let's take a closer look through the lens of 'values.' John's values are integrity, service, community, relationships, and wealth.

The company's new focus on high-profit margin products means that John is no longer selling what he believes to be the most beneficial product for the customer. He feels he is no longer servicing the client to the highest level. He feels out of integrity to be selling something that he believes to be worse for the customer, even though it means more profit for the company and a higher paycheck for John.

He felt great energy when they were in an open office with standing desks where all the sales reps could be in community with each other. Now that they put him in a private corner office, he has lost touch with that feeling of community.

Now that he only cold-calls new potential customers, any sales made are passed to another sales rep to cultivate the relationship. John feels distant from the relationships with customers that made him so excited to do his job.

The only one of his top career values that is still being met is 'wealth,' and it is only the fifth most important part of his career to him. Additionally, he now sees that the only way he can create more wealth is by selling a product that provides a disservice to the customers and leaves him feeling out of integrity. Not only is he violating some of his own values, there is also a conflict being created between his value of 'service' and his value of 'wealth'. Even if he makes more money than he ever has, he will feel conflicted about it.

This story might hit home for you as an employer or as something you have experienced in a job or career. When all of a sudden, the job that excited you in the past doesn't anymore, it's likely that it has to do with a mismatch with your values. One of the keys to understanding yourself better, aligning yourself with the best career for you, and creating energy and momentum in your life, is understanding and acting in alignment with your values.

For a condensed version of 'self-elicitation' of your values, use the questions around elicitation, Complex Equivalence, met, and violated that were in the previous exercises. Keep in mind that since values are often unconscious and one of our deepest levels of programming, a full elicitation is going to give you the most valuable insight to work with. To begin, using the self-elicitation questions can start you down the path of understanding yourself and others on a deeper level so you can have more motivation, more success in your communication, and work more effectively with others.

I'd like to touch on 'missing values' and 'conflicting values.' This can show up when someone is missing a key value necessary to align with what they want. In a career, it can show up for someone who is passionate about what they do and is simply not making any money. They could be missing a value around money completely. If you are running your own business and you want it to be profitable, it would be important that you have a value with some sort of financial component to it. It is not entirely uncommon for the value of money to either be at the bottom of someone's values or be missing altogether. This is a problem if you want to create an abundance of money through your career. Missing values can be added through techniques that work with the unconscious mind.

Having conflicting values can create its own kind of struggle. Imagine your number one value is 'giving,' and your number two value is 'creating wealth.' Depending on how you define those for yourself, there could be huge conflict, or they could support each other. If, for you, 'creating wealth' means amassing great fortunes and 'giving' means giving all of your income away, there's going to be quite the conflict for you. Reframing those values or integrating them will be key in aligning your energies internally. Otherwise, can you see how there will always be part of you striving to amass wealth while another part is trying to give everything away?

Worse yet, if you equate happiness with the expression of those two values, you'll continually be keeping happiness at arms-length. You might, for example, become frustrated with yourself. You might not understand why, when you have such a high income, you have never been able to build financial wealth. This is just one possible way that the conflict could show up.

Now you can start to see the depth of impact 'values' play in your life and that it isn't always just a matter of making different-ent conscious-level decisions. There are times when you absolute-ly must work with the unconscious mind. Both conflicting and missing values can be adjusted by working with someone who knows the NLP techniques around values.[6]

I trust that you now understand how valuable and vital values can be in empowering ourselves and how much of a factor they are in our perception.

Metaprograms

Something else that falls within our programming is Metaprograms. Metaprograms are the filters that people use consistently and often drive behavior. There are many of them; we'll just focus on a couple here.

The first we'll discuss is the 'toward vs. away' Metaprogram. If your filter is more 'toward' typically, it means moving toward pleasure is more motivating for you than moving away from pain. If most of your successful endeavors in life have been based on you focusing on the reward you will gain from accomplishing it, you likely work better with the 'toward' filter. It's useful to know how you set goals, the way you motivate yourself, and what kind of feedback helps you the most from others.

If your filter is more 'away' typically, moving away from pain is more motivating for you than moving toward pleasure. This filter is more common in our achievement-based society. For whatever reason, there does seem to be a correlation between suffering and excelling. It can be a very powerful 'away-from' motivator.

I could be slightly biased here because I have personally experienced this and seen it in many of the great humans I coach. I have also heard it thousands of times in various places in my life. The pattern is often running away from something by constantly improving and accomplishing the next thing.

For those that use suffering as their drive, it can become a secondary gain for not letting go of the belief or emotion that causes the suffering, a reason to hold on to it. They can believe that they will lose their drive or won't be successful without that suffering and pain. If you fall into this category, the question to ask yourself is, "how do you know?" How do you know that letting go of those old beliefs and emotions will cause you to lose your drive? What if this is actually holding your drive back? What if moving toward what you want without the suffering is the clean-burning fuel, and what you are currently using is toxic, flammable sludge? It may get the job done, yet at what cost?

Having coached, analyzed, and been around achievers most of

---

6   For a resource for finding an NLP Master Practitioner to work with, visit info@AIPonline.org.

my life, and also being one, I see firsthand the long-term costs and wear on the mind, emotions, body, and spirit of those who are fueling their success with the emotional baggage and limiting beliefs they are running from.

It works well in their 20s, and the only side effects are usually a little fatigue and an inability to settle.

Then, in their 30s and 40s it starts to show up in their physical health, or mental health, or in relationship strain. It looks like 'Mom or dad are too preoccupied to play with me', or 'why can't I ever just be', or 'what am I doing all this for anyway if I feel miserable'.

Then, as early as their 20s, but usually by late 40s or early 50s, the facade crumbles.

The soothing effect of the achievements or the movement or the external noise stops holding back the baggage and limiting beliefs.

The medicine turns out to have only been for symptoms. Sometimes it's worse than that. Sometimes the achiever finally gets the handful of things they thought they wanted in life. They were safe enough and placated on the path to them. Once they actually achieve them and realize it doesn't fix their emotional wounds or their limiting beliefs, the dam breaks. All of it comes flooding out, without anything that will mask the symptoms.

This is what is labeled as the "mid-life crisis". This is where the extreme changes happen on the surface. The cumulative strain and stress of those limiting beliefs and the emotional baggage have compounded. What started as a whisper is now screaming so loudly that it can't be avoided.

I'm not saying don't use your limiting beliefs and emotional baggage as fuel in the short-term. Just be aware that there are costs that come along with it.

I also wouldn't tell someone they can't use steroids to make them big and strong, but it would be unhelpful of me to not point out that there are consequences to the perceived short-term gains.

For those driven by limiting beliefs and emotional baggage, there is another way. A gentle, subtle way that takes a tremendous amount of courage.

What if, like Tarzan in the jungle or the trapeze artist, you step

What if, like Tarzan in the jungle or the trapeze artist, you step into the courage to swing out and let go of the suffering, to let go of what you are running from, trusting that something better and brighter will be there to catch you?

into the courage to swing out and let go of the suffering, to let go of what you are running from, trusting that something better and brighter will be there to catch you? Trust that it will be without the high cost your suffering has brought, that it will be something more fulfilling which will pull you forward.

Imagine what it will be like when you are pulled forward in life by what you are passionate about accomplishing. Imagine waking up excited to go accomplish because it's simply an expression of your wholeness, your creativity, your being. Imagine looking back to when you were using those negative emotions as fuel and realizing that they were terribly ineffective compared to what fuels you now. Remembering that all it took was courage and trust to let go of those things, believing the healthier drive of what would pull you forward would show up for you.

This moment of courage and trust is something I've experienced personally. I've seen it in myself, and I've seen the transformation first-hand in others. I've seen just how powerful it can be for someone to swing out to that uncertain place, trust themselves and life enough to let go of the pain and suffering that has been fueling them, and have faith that a new motivation will emerge to catch them and carry them above and beyond anything, and anywhere, their suffering could have gotten them.

Filtering By Self or Others

Another of the Metaprograms identifies whether someone filters things first 'by self' or first 'by others.' At one extreme end of the spectrum, someone can only look at everything based on how it affects them, their values and beliefs, and disregard others. At the other extreme, someone can only perceive events based on how they affect others or are seen by others and completely ignore themselves. Both extremes are unhealthy, and we'll look at each and a potential balance between them.

Let's first look at filtering 'by self', which aligns more with what is often labeled 'ego.' When I say ego, I mean the stereotypical person who always asks what's in it for them before they do anything. They talk only about what they are interested in and focus on their achievements and what they contributed. This is filtering 'by self' in an obvious way. It also might show up as someone lacking the awareness of others' emotions or nonverbal cues, such as someone else acting disinterested or annoyed with them.

Filtering 'by others,' you may not do new things because you are afraid that it might make others uncomfortable. When you do something good and are complimented, you immediately think about how you can compliment them back because you don't want them to feel left out. When you talk with others one-on-one or in a group, you think about the best way to help them, whether they are comfortable or if you need to rescue them from the topic on which they are about to say something silly.

Another form of filtering 'by others' that is detrimental is 'The Reverse-Ego.' The Reverse-Ego is where it seems as if you are filtering by 'others' in a way that is harmful to yourself. Make a mental note if any of these hit home for you.

- You may hyperfocus on how others see you.

- When you walk into a crowded room or a place with many people, you think and worry that everyone is watching you.

- You might be afraid to make the sales call because of how you will be perceived.

- You may not do new things because you are afraid to look silly or inexperienced to others.

- When you do something good and are complimented, you get uncomfortable because you don't want to seem self-centered.

- When you talk with others one-on-one or in a group, you worry about how your voice sounds or if what you're saying is interesting enough.

Do any of these ring a bell for you? Can you look back and see yourself doing them? This is a form of filtering by 'others' in an unhealthy way.

Note that neither filter is automatically better. Being completely unaware of others and cues from them isn't ideal, nor is being crippled by hyperawareness of what is perceived in others. There is a balance between the two that is most effective.

Here's an example of a balance between the two. You are focused on truly seeing who others are on a deeper level. When you walk into a crowded room or a place with many people, you think about what others might be thinking or feeling from a place of awareness, not what it might mean about you. You maintain awareness of how you feel, separate from others. You consider who might benefit from a conversation with you or who you might know that you can connect them with to help them accomplish their goals, and you also consider who you want to connect with that you'll most enjoy conversation with. You might be thinking about how you can make the person on the other end of your sales call make the best choice for themselves regarding your product or service, regardless of if you get the sale or how you will be perceived. Even though you think of others, you always are aware of what you are looking for in relationships and conversations. You hold healthy boundaries and won't tolerate prolonged poor treatment by others, and you won't do things that cause harm and anguish to yourself just because it might be beneficial to others.

As you can tell from the previous examples, the Reverse-Ego is the subtle side of the ego. It focuses on the self through filtering 'by others' in ways that seem to be the opposite of the stereotypical ego. It is ego in disguise because it shows up as 'anti-ego.' Outright ego is much easier to recognize and is thus easier to change. The Reverse-Ego can be stealthily damaging to us and our interactions with others because of how much of the time it goes unnoticed. The next time you are walking through a crowded place, are speaking on stage, or are talking with someone and you think people are staring at you or judging your speech or thinking your voice sounds funny, acknowledge that is your ego showing up, and also remember that they have an ego that influences their perception, too. It is equally as likely that the crowd never noticed you, that they were looking at their phone instead of listening to your speech, or that they didn't hear a word you said because they were trying to remember what their partner asked them to get at the grocery store or were worrying if the outfit they chose was too unprofessional. Remember that your experience is dictated by your beliefs and perception and choose a belief that empowers your experience.

Ego can be such a touchy subject and a word with a lot of stigmas. If you do experience a lot of the Reverse-Ego scenarios mentioned, notice how you react to the stereotypical ego label. There is often a correlation between those that exhibit Reverse-Ego tendencies and those who have a negative knee-jerk reaction to the overt ego.

As we discussed regarding the 'Shadow,' be cautious of what you toss away into the 'not-me' category. Do you catch yourself thinking, "Egotistical? That is not me! I am not that way!"

These things have a way of hiding from our perception, and what we aren't aware of often has control over us. As for the ego, it is actually a vital part of us being able to exist on this planet and communicate with each other. It is what allows us to be functional members of society. It is not about the elimination of the ego. If you have ever had an experience where your ego truly disappears temporarily, you will know just how important it is in daily functioning. Instead, it is about balance and having a symbiotic relationship with your ego. It's about being able to balance filtering 'by self' and filtering 'by others' in a way that is empowering to all.

Chapter 8

Thoughts

The Narrator

Who narrates your thoughts? Who is behind that little voice in your head that talks to you all the time? Is it you? Is it your voice? If so, is it always you, or is there some other voice that sometimes pops in?

Our thoughts are generated by our programming: our beliefs and values, among other things. The majority of those thoughts are habitual and unconscious. If the thoughts are generated by your programming and running in the background, is that voice really yours?

If you identify with your thoughts and equate them with being you, it's hard not to be affected deeply by them. Instead, can you see your thoughts as clues that lead you back to programming that needs an update? Alternatively, can you simply let those thoughts come and go, floating across the surface of your mind and drifting away without any response to them? You can reclaim precious energy and power by updating your programming to change the thoughts to more empowering ones or by allowing the thoughts to float by without resistance from you.

Stop from time to time and really listen to the voice in your head. You may find this tricky because when you really stop and focus on it, the voice often stops. Let the meaning of that sink in. When your narrator is talking, mentally stop and ask, "who is talking right now" and notice what you experience.

As you become more consciously aware of your narrator, let it lead you to the areas that can be improved. It is especially helpful to find situations that can pull out the narrator. You've probably heard that communication is 55% body language, 38% tonality, and only 7% the words that we use. Therefore, any form of written communication is going to cause our programming to reach out and interpret the vast majority of what isn't being communicated. When you get an email or text message, whose voice does the reading? It may sound like the other person, yet you are actually listening to the narrator in your own head. Are there consistent themes in the attitudes or intentions you interpret from others? It's easy to forget that it isn't actually the person on the other end of the text or email sounding like that. It is your narrator's interpretation of how they are saying it. Indeed, when reading an email or text message, there's more of 'you' in it than the person who actually typed the words.

Have you ever caught yourself having hypothetical conversations with someone else in your mind? Have you noticed that sometimes during those fictional conversations, you get more and more upset, defensive, or justified? Maybe it's right before you pick up the phone to make sales calls, or as you think about how you'll respond to the voicemail your mother left you. Maybe it's in preparation for confronting your teenager about what you found in their sock drawer. In the conversation in your head, when you hear the other person arguing with you, being difficult, or chastising you, who is really doing the talking? The other person in this conversation isn't actually in your head, so anything this person says to you in your mind is actually coming from you. So, instead of only responding to them in the moment of the actual conversation, you are responding to all the things they never said as well. Even in the moment of the real conversation, you are often still having more of a conversation with yourself than you are with them. Seems kind of unfair to them, doesn't it? In summary, there is more to learn about you as you observe the qualities and responses you give your mental construct of them than there is to learn about them.

If, by chance, everyone angers you by email or text, that might tell you something. If that's the case, what is it about how the narrator is talking to you that is upsetting? What meaning is being given that isn't actually present in the text being read to you by your narrator? These are all little clues to help you go deeper into your own perception and become more aware. If you are constantly defensive, there's a good chance your narrator lays the judgment on thick. If you are often angry, there's a decent possibility your narrator has a challenging or irking way of communicating with you. And who could irritate or hurt you more than your narrator who has been there with you since the beginning? It knows all your buttons to push, all of your sensitivities and insecurities.

Since this voice, and your thoughts overall, are the bridge between your programming and what feelings you have, it is imperative that you learn as much as possible about your own thought patterns and dig deeper into the make-up of your own narrator, if you are to move forward toward empowerment.

Anxiety or Positive Anticipation (Excitement)

What's the difference between anxiety and positive anticipation? Think about when you have experienced anxiety and when you were really excited before a big event. Maybe it was sports in school or some sort of performance. Where in your body did those two show up? Physiologically, they are nearly identical. It is the meaning you attached that made the feeling positive or negative and changed your experience of the situation.

If we are excited about something in the future, we typically imagine a positive outcome. When we feel anxious, it tends to be because we are thinking of a negative future outcome or a series of negatively focused 'what-ifs'.

Take something you are currently anxious about. Now, imagine what you were anxious about as a huge success instead. In your mind, go to a time after the event you were anxious about has reached a successful conclusion. Where did the anxiety go? That's right; it's gone. As long as you imagine a positive outcome, the anxiety will disappear. Since the mind can't tell the difference between a vividly imagined outcome and one that happens in real life, anxiety is typically created based on future-based fearful thoughts. The body then responds to the mind and creates a sensation, and the mind interprets that sensation as affirmation that the anxiety is real, creating an anxiety loop. It isn't the events themselves that cause the anxiety; it's the way we imagine them playing out. This is exciting because it means we have so much more power over our anxiety than we might have previously realized.

Let's delve deeper into the 'what-ifs'. Think about these negative thoughts:

- What if they don't like me?

- What if I get fired?

- What if I die young?

By listening to these thoughts, they take us down the path of assuming they are true. The answer to a 'what-if' causes us to start thinking about what would happen next or what it would mean if it did happen. Let's turn that on its head. What if we gave ourselves positive 'what-ifs'?

- What if the one sale turns into three?

- What if I have an amazing time at the party?

- What if the date I'm going on today is my future spouse?

- What if that next big opportunity for me shows up today?

How would your day-to-day experience change if you imagined positive outcomes for future events and turned your negative 'what-ifs' into positive ones? Turn "what if they don't like me" into "what if they absolutely love me." It causes you to go down the path of what happens next, assuming that they love you. Now you are creating a positive emotional response based on the thought of them loving you. For a couple more, turn "what if I get fired" into "what if they promote me" and "what if I die young" to "what if I live to a hundred with full health." This shows the power of perception. Changing the question leads us down an entirely different path and creates a new experience.

Become more consciously aware of your 'what-ifs' and turn them around. Make it your new habit, and notice what changes appear in your emotional states and experience of life. You could choose to move on from this section without making a note of this. You could easily keep reading and not set a reminder for yourself for the next 30 days to change your 'what-ifs'. You could read this and change nothing. Then again, what if you did?"

Chapter 9

Feelings/Emotions

Emotions are fascinating. They are like the color of life. A life without any emotions has a bland, gray feel to it. So if we know that emotions are important to a full experience and quality of life, then we must explore how to have them work to our advantage.

Response Out of Proportion to the Event

There is a common assumption that gives away power in our experience. The assumption is that emotions just happen, and we don't have control over them. Most people do not believe that on a logical and conscious level, yet it shows in our actions. Think of any time when you have the thoughts:

- "They made me mad."

- "That event made me sad."

- "That experience made me happy."

Notice that while most people would say that we do have control over our emotions, we often behave as if we don't have control. If we behave as if something is making us feel a certain emotion, then our power is in the hands of whatever made us feel that way. We're also assuming that there is a cause-and-effect relationship where we are 'at effect' to whatever caused us to experience the emotion. The event or person is the cause, and our emotional response is the effect. For example, someone cuts me off on the road, which causes me to feel angry automatically.

There is another crucial step to consider.

- Step one, the person cuts me off on the road.

- Step two, I give that event meaning.

- Step three, I respond appropriately to the meaning I have given it.

For the sake of simplicity, I've categorized this into three steps. There are many sub-steps happening on the unconscious level, yet the three steps are enough for our purposes here so that we can recognize where we are giving away our control and power.

If you know of someone who is very emotional and seems to be upset by things that don't make sense or where their emotional response is out of proportion to the event, then they are most likely viewing this multi-step process as only two steps. By "response out of proportion to the event," I mean our response is greater than the event that is supposedly causing it. This will become clearer in the example shortly. Remember, most people do not emotionally respond inappropriately to the meaning they have given the event. They are more often creating a meaning to the event which is out of proportion, which turns into a response that is out of proportion. In simpler terms, it is the meaning they've given the event that is distorted, and they are reacting appropriately to that meaning.

Let's look at an example: Brenda is in a relationship with Dan. They have been dating for a few weeks, and Dan isn't much for texting. Brenda, on the other hand, always has her phone in her hand. One day, Dan goes more than an hour without responding to Brenda's texts. Brenda becomes angry and tells Dan he doesn't care about her because he won't respond back quickly, so they might as well break it off now.

Let's look at what is happening here. The response is clearly out of proportion to the event. Brenda's reaction to breaking off the relationship because of his lack of response for an hour seems a little extreme. Now let's break down the three steps.

- Step one, Dan doesn't respond for over an hour.

- Step two, Brenda takes that to mean that she clearly isn't important to Dan, that she is bothering him, and that anything else he says is just leading her on because he doesn't care about her.

- Step three, she responds somewhat appropriately to the huge meaning she has attached to the event of Dan not responding for over an hour.

Let's pause the story momentarily and break step two into substeps. We revisit T. Harv Eker's PTFAR: Programming, Thoughts, Feelings, Actions, Results.

The emotional response we've been discussing falls into the category of feelings. Feelings (emotions) are preceded by thoughts, which are preceded by our programming. Our programming is where our values and beliefs lie. This means that if we revise the 2nd step above, we can say that the event passes through our perceptual filter of values and beliefs, which allows us to generate thoughts based on seeing the event through those filters. So, the new process becomes:

Event → Beliefs & Values → Thoughts → Emotional Response

Now back to Brenda. Let's go further into her backstory.

Brenda has only recently gotten out of a relationship where her ex-boyfriend, Paul, would constantly stay out late and not respond to her. When she would confront him about it, he'd brush her off and tell her it was none of her business, that she was just being needy, and that he had more important priorities than keeping her informed on his every move.

When Brenda was in high school, she had a close friend whom she texted with all day long. One weekend, her friend suddenly stopped texting her. She found out two days later that her friend had died in a car crash.

When Brenda was in college, she dated a guy who she would text and who wouldn't respond for over an hour each time. One day, she overheard him telling his buddies that he wasn't interested, he didn't like their conversations, that she was starting to annoy him, and that Brenda clearly couldn't take the hint.

Now let's go back to Dan and his lack of response. When you mix together Brenda's past experiences, it makes sense why she would create the meaning she did from Dan not responding. And, when you think about the meaning given, doesn't her emotional response seem appropriate? If you had a friend who texted you every 5 minutes that suddenly died, and you linked the experience of her death to a lack of response, then you combined that with a past boyfriend who showed a lack of caring through his response times, and then you combined both of those things with the experience of humiliation that she was dull and annoying to someone based on texting, then her emotional response seems reasonable.

The challenge is that Brenda isn't aware of any of this. She doesn't even know that she is filtering the event. Brenda sees it as simply "the" event. She thinks that when someone doesn't text for that long, it automatically means those things. She makes the mistake of thinking that the action means the same thing to Dan and, thus, must be intentional.

Brenda goes on to have a long string of short relationships that often end in the same way as her relationship with Dan did. She eventually takes the meanings of the texting scenario and her experiences with dating and makes a disempowering generalization. Brenda decides her past experiences mean that none of the guys she dates care about her and that none of them are trustworthy. Time reinforces her distortions further, enabling her to adopt the belief that since all of the guys she has dated have been this way, it means that all guys don't care about her. After a while, she even adds the belief that no guys are trustworthy. This pattern goes on to affect not just her dating relationships, but any relationship with a male. She is constantly seeking to find actions of men that are untrustworthy and signs that they don't care about her. Through that perceptual filter, of course, she can find them. It affects her friendships, too. She constantly hints to her friends that their boyfriends might be cheating on them and that they shouldn't be trusted, causing her friends to avoid her. In school, her professor doesn't respond quickly enough to her emailed question, proving that he doesn't care about her, so she drops his class.

On the one hand, this is a somewhat extreme example. On the other hand, this is happening all day, every day around you, and also within you. I guarantee that somewhere in your life, possibly many places, you are automatically responding to events based on the meanings you have attached to them, meanings that you are unaware of. Awareness is a vital key in regaining and maintaining empowerment in life.

Positively Influencing Our Emotional State

Now that we have discussed the idea that the meaning we give an event is what we are really responding to, let's look at how to use this to empower ourselves and our experience of life.

Imagine you are driving down the road, and someone cuts you off. It upsets you. Is the source of your upset that the other person cut you off? It depends. Yes, we can put the blame on the external part, in this instance, the person who cut you off. We can look externally for the solution and tell ourselves, "other people shouldn't do that." Yet, if we blame the external, there's a subtle shift of control being given away here. You are giving control of your emotions and experience of the situation to someone else. Now let's look at the internal part. The last time someone cut you off, what was the meaning you gave it? What judgments did you throw at the perpetrator, and how did you react based on those judgments? What were you focused on? Was it how their action impacted you or curiosity as to what must be so important that they would cut someone off?

Step into a hypothetical mindset for a moment: Someone just cut you off. The other driver just imposed on your precious driving space. "What is wrong with them? They must be so inconsiderate. I bet they do this all the time just because they think they can. They think they are so important that they can just cut other people off and completely disregard them. Maybe someone should teach them a lesson. I should tailgate them and aggressively honk because they did this to me, and that's what they deserve. I'm in the right here because actions bring consequences, and this jerk can't keep doing this to everyone else. If I don't teach them a lesson, then who will? I bet they saw me and intentionally cut me off just because they could. I mean, that's what jerks do. I bet they thought I looked like an easy target to cut off."

Now step into another hypothetical inner dialogue. Someone just cut you off: Woah, that startled me. Did I not see them wanting to get over? They must be having a rough day. I bet they're late for work. That always stresses me out when I'm late for work. I bet they didn't even see me. They might be late for work after being up all night with a newborn. And they could have just lost their spouse, so they are all alone in their parenting. Wow, what a struggle. My heart goes out to them. On top of that, they could be the sole caregiver for their grandparent, who is completely dependent upon them. They might have already been late twice, and if they are late again, they will get fired. Then, they would be stuck caring for a newborn and an aging grandparent without any help or a job. I hope they make it on time.

The second version may be a little far-fetched, yet it doesn't actually matter which version of events is true. What matters is that your experience is determined by which version of the story you tell yourself in that situation. We almost never find out the truth, yet we behave as if we know. Our actions in those situations show us whether we were attaching a positive or negative meaning to it. Both had the outer event of being cut off. For one, that event turned into a negative experience. For the other, it became a way to experience empathy and possibly gratitude for one's own life as a result.

So, what actually was the problem? The actual event was the same in both scenarios. The difference between the two was the story and meaning given to it, creating different emotional states and experiences as a result. If the experience is changed so much by the meaning we give to it, then it can't just be the event that is the problem. It has to be deeper than that. In all situations, it is this formula: event + (meaning, story, emotions) = experience. This goes for every single experience that you have in your entire life. Every. Single. One. To gloss over this is a disservice to your empowerment and your experience of life. Now it's time for you to get real with yourself. It's time for you to experience this with an exercise.

- Use the blank diagram and fill in the original event information from a recent experience that ended in a negative emotional state or response.

- Put the same event in the 'Positive Alternative' box, then add other possible positive meanings in the 'Meaning' box. If you can't find any, phone a friend. Because, we can always find a positive meaning.

- Finally, write out the appropriate experience, emotional state, or response based on the meaning you gave it.

- Reach up really high with one hand, bend your arm at the elbow, and pat yourself on the back. You have just empowered yourself by creating a positive experience from what used to be a negative experience.

- Rinse and repeat as many times as you'd like to feel more empowered.

*** Caution: doing this exercise means that you'll be taking ownership and losing the crutch of having something or someone else to blame as the cause of your negative experience/response. This practice can be tough at first, though once mastered, it can be intensely rewarding.

Understanding yourself, your relationship with your emotions, what your perception is made of, and how to make subtle shifts in it will help you empower yourself more than any external accomplishment ever could.

	Event	Meaning	Experience (Emotional State/Response)
Original Event	Dan doesn't text me for over an hour	Something is wrong. I'm not important to him. He doesn't care about me. He thinks I'm annoying.	I get angry and break off the relationship. Dan was the problem. Men are a problem. Why does this always happen to me?
Positive Alternative	Dan doesn't text me for over an hour	He must be in an important meeting. I know he loves me and would rather spend time with me, yet he loves me so much that he's off working hard to help support our financial goals and dreams.	I surprise him at work for lunch so we can spend a little more time together.

	Event	Meaning	Experience (Emotional State/Response)
Original Event			
Positive Alternative			

Finding Baggage

Baggage is a term used here to mean any emotions carried from the past that aren't serving us or beliefs that limit us. As discussed earlier, they can cause our response to be out of proportion to the event. Becoming more aware of when a response isn't proportional is a great tool for empowering ourselves. With unconscious work and emotional release work, and shifting our perception to be more empowering, 'disproportionate responses' are guides to healing. If we get overly angry in a situation that doesn't call for that level of anger, then our response is pointing us to the emotional baggage that can be resolved and will improve our experience of life. If the same event can happen to two different people with different emotional responses from each of them, then we know that the emotional response tells us more about the person responding than about the event.

> *If the same event can happen to two different people with different emotional responses from each of them, then we know that the emotional response tells us more about the person responding than about the event.*

The same is true of a disproportionate response to an event, where it tells us more about ourselves than the event. The event is simply the stimulus. If you feel extremely guilty about something that doesn't warrant that level of guilt, you can search within yourself to find out what is causing you to respond with guilt when it is unnecessary or unhelpful. We've gone through some of these causes throughout this book. It could be early childhood emotional experiences, modeling emotions you learned from parents or others, extreme emotional events at any point in your life, accidental attachment of negative meaning to certain events, a distorted sense of self-worth, a distorted self-perception, or other possibilities.

Out-of-proportion emotional responses can be a benefit if you choose. They can surface baggage that is ready for resolution. They can provide opportunities to resolve old emotions or beliefs that no longer serve you. Each time you let an old emotion or belief go, you take another step toward your own empowerment and improving your experience of life. Since these emotional responses show up frequently for most people, this is a great opportunity. You can choose which way to observe your own emotional responses moving forward. You can choose that your emotions must be caused by the event, and therefore you need to change something about the event or stay away from those kinds of events. Alternatively, you can choose to be aware of your responses and look for places where your response indicates an opportunity for emotional growth.

Allow me to shake you gently awake. You've been asleep at the wheel, with automatic emotional responses to events in your life happening outside of your awareness. You don't need to climb Mount Everest to empower yourself. It can happen one small, simple decision at a time. Understanding yourself, your relationship with your emotions, what your perception is made of, and how to make subtle shifts in it will help you empower yourself more than any external accomplishment ever could. How much growth and progress in your empowerment could you make by simply becoming aware of your own emotional responses?

The Chicken and the Egg

Using PTFAR is an incredible way to create empowering change in your life. When we have the right beliefs, they cultivate the supporting thoughts, which support empowering emotions, putting us into the right actions, and giving us the results we want. Occasionally, even when we have worked with the beliefs and thoughts and know what we need to do, we can still struggle with aligning the feelings to support the action. We can address the programming and thoughts to shift the feeling, and still not quite get there.

This struggle is where the chicken and the egg analogy comes in. Many people who don't do something they meant to do will say something along the lines of not having the motivation to do it. "I didn't feel like doing it" is a good example of this. This can be overcome. Let me demonstrate with an example.

"When I have the right mindset, I do the activity."

- Take an area in your life where you believe this is true. One possibility is, "when I feel motivated to work out, I go to the gym and work out."

- Now, reverse the sentence. "When I go to the gym and work out, I feel motivated to work out."

- Is it also true? If so, celebrate.

This is a way of increasing your chances of accomplishing what you want, even when you don't feel like it, by reminding yourself that after you do it, you'll have the feeling you were seeking to get you into action. It creates a positive spiral. When you start with the feeling, and it isn't working, start with the action instead. This approach empowers you to take consistent action in that area by eliminating the need for a certain emotional state as a precursor to the action. You can also use this as a shortcut to get into action quickly and buy yourself time to continue to work on your beliefs, thoughts, and emotions.

Throughout this section, we have looked at the role emotions play in your empowerment, how to positively influence your emotional state, and how to work around your emotions even when they aren't aligned with the actions you want to take. We've done an exercise to confirm that your emotions have more to do with how you filter an event than the event itself.

Now, let's go deeper into one of the barriers to changing your perception we discussed earlier and more tools to help in your empowerment.

Part 3

Transforming your Perception

Chapter 10

Changing Disempowering Perceptions

Secondary Gain

We briefly discussed 'secondary gain' at the beginning of this book. As a reminder, 'secondary gain' is when you are gaining a perceived positive benefit from a negative, such as a negative behavior, belief, or emotion. 'Secondary gain' is one of the biggest obstacles to change when preparing ourselves to let go of baggage. When we are benefitting from a problem, it gives our unconscious mind a reason to hold on to it. In successfully changing beliefs or emotions at the unconscious level, the unconscious mind must realize that either the gain isn't worth holding on to the emotional baggage or that we can get that gain in a better way, which also allows us to let go of the baggage.

> *When we are benefitting from a problem, it gives our unconscious mind a reason to hold on to it.*

Here's an example to illustrate 'secondary gain.' Jim has been a busy person all of his life. He has several degrees and multiple professional licenses and has done well in business. Jim has had success in nearly every professional endeavor he has attempted. People around him often wonder how Jim gets it all done. On top of the business, he has a big family and attends every sports event for his children. He is in constant motion and always on to the next thing. He never says no to any request, and his business clients have given him rave reviews for his level of service.

The problem is that he is tired. It's not that he won't slow down. He can't. He has started to notice that, while he is physically there for everything for his family and business, he is rarely mentally and emotionally present. He has an endless to-do list that he continues to add to compulsively. His health has taken a back seat, as well.

Jim has begun to realize that he doesn't want life just to be one big blur of accomplishments, so he has come to a practitioner that specializes in NLP and MER®. After exploring it together, they discover that Jim has a limiting belief of "I'm not enough" that came from his childhood. He had a great childhood, yet his father was always very busy, and he didn't get much attention. The only time he did was when Jim would do something exceptional in school or sports. Jim inadvertently took on this belief and a corresponding one of "if I accomplish enough, I'll receive attention and love," and his unconscious mind held on to it.

Now that he understands one of the deep beliefs fueling his constant motion, he wants to let it go. The only problem is that he fears losing his drive if he lets go of the belief. He worries that so many of his accomplishments have been because of his unconscious efforts to prove he is enough. This is his 'secondary gain.' While Jim is realizing that this belief is stealing the quality and presence out of his relationships and his life, the belief has also fueled his success for him. He is afraid to lose this gain if he lets go of the belief. The belief will remain intact if the gain isn't dealt with first.

As Jim works with the 'secondary gain,' he must begin believing on the conscious and unconscious level that he can find other, better ways to get the same result. If Jim can get to the point of being able to let go of "I'm not enough" while believing he will have a healthier, more purposeful drive to accomplish the things he wants to accomplish, then he has reframed the 'secondary gain' and can let go of the belief that is limiting the quality of his life.

The more you begin to notice the gain that comes from any less-than-ideal behavior, the faster you'll be able to change how you choose to behave positively. As a bonus, it helps you stay out of judgment of yourself and others. Suppose you start to see the possibility that Sally consistently drinking too much at the office party is gaining her the benefit of not feeling the social anxiety she often gets. That view can change your perception of her behavior. As we discussed earlier in the book, people are not their behavior.

That includes Jim, Sally, and of course, you.

Now, it's your turn. What are the things in your life that have 'secondary gain'? It could be that:

- You talk about your problems a lot, and that gives you more attention.

- You gossip about others often, which makes those around you always want to come to you to get the juicy details of office drama.

- You drink too much in social settings, and that makes you feel less afraid or self-conscious.

Write out a few unwanted behaviors you have and what the 'secondary gain' of them might be.

_____

_____

_____

Now that you've created more awareness of potential 'secondary gains,' let's continue.

NLP and MER® Techniques

Psychologist Nathaniel Branden said, "The first step toward change is awareness. The second step is acceptance." We cannot purposefully change something if we are unaware of it. And, if we reject what we become aware of, we lose the power to change it. Once we empower ourselves by accepting what we become aware of, then we are primed for positive change.

If you have identified a belief that limits you, an emotion that isn't serving you, or something in your perception causing more harm than good, we can now use NLP and MER® tools and techniques to release it. I want to share a few of these techniques you can use at any time for yourself. Some of them are subtle or geared toward the unconscious mind, and some are more surface-level. All can be useful in making positive changes to your perception. This section will move through the tools quickly, so take what's useful for you and ask yourself how you can implement it in your own life.

Reframing

Most of what we have discussed in this book involves 'reframing.' It is simple and also incredibly powerful. The exercise example of Dan not texting back for over an hour is an example of a 'meaning reframe.' A 'meaning reframe' is when we change the meaning of the action or stimuli. If you are frustrated with your relationship and isolate that the issue stems from the meaning you give your partner's behavior, then a meaning reframe may be helpful. Yes, your partner can change their behavior, and that's the external change, yet you don't have any control over that. At all times, you do have the power to examine and change the meaning you give that behavior.

For example, your partner never makes dinner for you. You realize that you are deciding that your partner not making dinner means they don't appreciate you. As much as you might like to think you can, you cannot actually read anyone's mind. There are many other possible meanings that you could take from your partner not making dinner. Maybe your partner isn't aware that not making dinner gives the impression that they don't care. Maybe they think you get enjoyment from cooking dinner, and they don't want to take that away from you. Maybe they grew up modeling their parents, thinking that a certain partner in a relationship always cooked. Maybe they are self-conscious about their cooking because a previous partner harshly criticized their cooking ability, and they are afraid to cook for someone else.

Of course, directly asking them, coming from curiosity, can help you understand at a deeper level, but at certain times in life, we may not be able to verify what is really going on in their mind. And yet, whether something external can change or not, you always have the power to change or reframe the meaning you choose to assign.

Whether we like it or not, the most painful and extreme circumstances we experience have a big impact on shaping our lives. Life happens. That is a fact. The hardest part to accept is that, ultimately, the things that happen have no inherent meaning. It is our choice how we perceive them. We give events their meaning, and that becomes our reality. We can choose to be controlled by them

The hardest part to accept is that, ultimately, the things that happen have no inherent meaning. It is our choice how we perceive them.

and see them negatively, or we can choose to use them as a catalyst for our personal growth or confirmation that we are on the right path.

You already have used reframing in several exercises in this book. The exercise earlier of seeing your life as happening to you or happening for you is one of them.

Now, go back to this exercise, take a few of your responses, and write them again here. Write down the 3 most painful things that have happened to you in your life:

_____

_____

_____

As we know, there is great power in our darkest moments if we choose to use them for our empowerment and write the positive reframe of them. Rewrite your three things in an empowering way:

_____

_____

_____

We are all on this journey of life together. In my own discovery of the Power of Perception, I have done these exercises, too. Here are a few of my own examples. Notice if any of them connect with your experience.

(Before Reframe)

• Struggle with depression and purposelessness led to dark times and heavy shame and guilt.

• Struggle with those feelings led me to addictive habits, which led me to decreased self-worth, self-loathing, shame, and unworthiness.

• Being able to read others well and needing others to behave in certain ways for me to feel happy or feel like I'm enough led me to be manipulative of others and feel inauthentic.

(After Reframe)

- My Shame, inauthenticity, and self-loathing led to a high enough level of suffering to push me headfirst into areas of self-awareness and growth.

- Depression, anxiety, and purposelessness led me to understand them and find power over them, leading me to Neuro-Linguistic Programming, Mental and Emotional Release®, and a vast number of other resources.

- Because of all of those resources and growth, I am able to help others who are striving to empower themselves.

It is because of all of my human struggle, not in spite of it, that I am able to write this book, work one-on-one with others, be a resource to anyone in my world, and do it in a way that deeply moves me and creates massive purpose in my life.

There is only one difference between the 'to version' of our stories and the 'for version.' The way we choose to perceive our experiences is this singular difference that creates a never-ending spiral of suffering or an incredible level of empowerment. I want to pause here and acknowledge your courage to do this exercise. I trust you are finding this as great of a tool in the journey to empowerment as I have.

Before we go to 'context reframing,' I want to look at a fun exercise in 'reframing.'

Proving the Impossible Possible

"The limits of the possible can only be defined by going beyond them into the impossible." - Arthur C. Clarke

What is impossible for you? It could be running a marathon, climbing Mount Everest, doing a silent retreat, or completing a 3-day fast. It also could be not drinking alcohol for a month straight, asking someone out on a date, or applying for that promotion. Use the next few lines and write out everything you can think of that is impossible for you:

_____

_____

_____

Now order those from 'most impossible' to 'just beyond possible:'

_____

_____

_____

_____

_____

Great! Now we have a list of the things that are impossible for you in order of impossibility. Read this next paragraph and then close your eyes for a moment.

Imagine that you just completed the number one most impossible thing on your list. Go there in your mind and see, hear, feel, taste, and smell it happening. Do whatever makes it most real for you. Now think about the rest of your list. You've just proved, beyond the shadow of a doubt, that what you believed impossible is possible for you. Give this 60 seconds, and close your eyes.

What does this mean for the rest of your list? What does this mean for the things you consider big challenges on a daily basis? There's only one way to find out. Choose an item from your list. What does accomplishing something you previously thought impossible do for your experience of things you already know are possible?

Here's some accidental wisdom that sums this up from the television series "How I Met Your Mother:"

Barney Stinson: "All my life I have dared to go past what is possible."

Interviewer (Barney): "To the impossible?"

Barney Stinson: "Actually, past that. To the place where the possible and the impossible meet, to become... the 'possimpible'."

Context Reframing

Another type of reframing is 'context reframing.' 'Context reframing' is another specific way we can change the way we see behavior based on changing the context where it appears.

We can do this by asking, "In what other context (situation) would this behavior be a positive one?"

One example is a strong-willed child. When your child is

strong-willed, continually asks why, and doesn't concede to your demands, a 'context reframe' can help you change how you look at their behavior instead of feeling the need to demand them to change. When your child is out of school and on their own, do you want them to accept or give in to others' demands blindly? Do you want them to do that in their relationships or their career? Probably not. If we look at it in one context, it is a frustrating behavioral problem. In another, it is an empowering and desirable trait. Your two-year-old's endless passion for fearlessly climbing everything they can reach may be stressful now, yet having a bold, persistent, and adventurous child when they are thirty is an entirely different context to consider. Another way to change your perception of a problematic belief is called Cartesian Coordinates. Go with me on this. Let's skip the explanation of what it is and do a quick exercise with it. I included possible answers to help you understand the questions, as they can seem strange at first. If you just let go and trust your unconscious mind as you go through the exercise, you'll find it easy to answer these questions.

Let's use the belief "my relationships are all terrible" as an example:

- What would happen if you did believe your relationships are all terrible?

(...then every time I date someone, it would fall apart)
- What would happen if you didn't believe your relationships are all terrible?

(...I could start to see it as possible for me to have a great relationship)
- What wouldn't happen if you did believe your relationships are all terrible?

(...then I wouldn't ever find love)
- What wouldn't happen if you didn't believe your relationships are all terrible?

(...then I wouldn't ignore the great qualities in the relationships I already have)

The main thing to know about Cartesian Coordinates is that they are simply allowing a change in the way you are looking at the problem, which causes the problem to change or disappear.

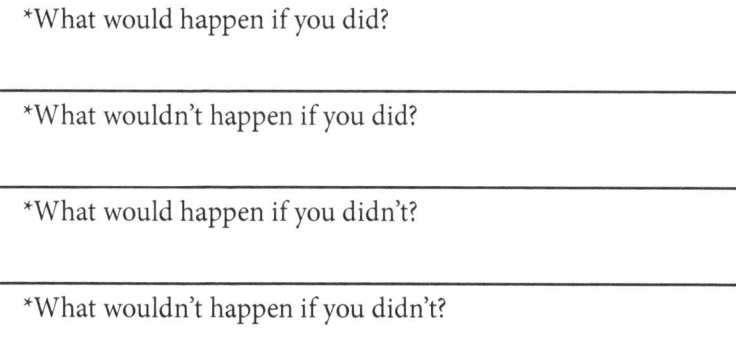

*What would happen if you did?

_____

*What wouldn't happen if you did?

_____

*What would happen if you didn't?

_____

*What wouldn't happen if you didn't?

_____

Working with Common Fears

There are some fears that tend to be the most common. Let's take these fears and have some fun with them. Pay close attention to any of these fears that you feel you have. After reading each section, feel free to use the Cartesian Coordinates questions above on each of the fears, along with the questions from "It's a good thing to not know" earlier in the book (also referenced in the back of the book in Tools & Exercises section).

Fear of Failure

You say you fear failure, yet what is failure? First, you must define it.

- Is it failure when you expected to succeed and didn't?

- If you change or remove your expectation, can you make failure impossible?

- Is it failure when someone else expected you to succeed and you didn't?

- If so, who is this "someone else"? Is it anyone else, or a specific group of people?

- If a two-year-old says you failed, do you believe them?

- What about someone your age?

Winston Churchill defines it in this way, "Success consists of going from failure to failure without loss of enthusiasm." Isn't failure simply a matter of perspective? If so, it means you can shift your perspective until failure no longer exists. You can reframe the meaning, or you can reframe it to another context where it would be considered success. What is failure? What is it not? How do you know what it is not? What do you need to not know to know this? Confused? Perfect. Now you've set yourself up for success.

Fear of Rejection

- What is your definition of rejection?

- How do you know when you're being rejected?

- Has it ever happened to someone else, and they didn't see it as rejection?

That would be impossible if rejection were a fixed thing. Therefore, it must be fluid. It must be based on your perception and your definition. Is someone saying no to you the same as rejection? Can anyone reject you without your permission? Or do they create the stimuli and you determine the response? Change the meaning, and the response automatically changes. What would you have to choose to believe about yourself in order to never reject yourself based on stimuli from the outside world again?

Fear of Inadequacy

You fear inadequacy. You fear you aren't good enough. Enough? Enough compared to what? Let's first clarify what enough would look like.

- Is adequacy on a scale, and if you drop below a certain number, you become inadequate?

- Is it pass/fail, all-or-nothing?

- Is only one person at a time on the planet enough, and everyone else isn't?

Go find an example of someone who is enough and find out the formula.

- How do they know they are enough and are they enough based on your opinion or theirs?

- What if they think they aren't enough, and you think they are?

- What if they think they are enough, and you think they aren't?

- Who would be right in those cases?

If you don't have an answer, then you have created an unsolvable riddle. What a clever little trickster of an ego you have. Wondering if you are enough or believing that you aren't without knowing what enough is, makes no sense. You're wondering how many apples it takes to kick a homerun, and you are afraid you are the problem, not your question. Keep pushing that boulder up the hill. Are you Sisyphus? Or are you the boulder, the hill, or gravity itself?

Fear of Uncertainty

You say you fear uncertainty. Do you drive a car? Have you ever driven on a two-lane road with cars coming in the other direction? At any moment, one of them could come across the lane and hit you, so if you've ever had a moment where you weren't terrified while driving, you've embraced uncertainty. That means you can recreate that feeling. Fear of uncertainty is only contextual.

Let's make a world where uncertainty doesn't exist! You know exactly what will happen every moment of every day for the rest of your life. How long would it take for you to be begging for just one thing to happen that you weren't expecting? This means you love uncertainty in certain contexts. If you can find those contexts, then you can find out what it is about them that makes you embrace uncertainty and use it to release your fear.

Fear of uncertainty is only contextual.

What's the difference between the uncertainty you can't handle and the uncertainty you love?

Fear of Missing Out

Do you fear missing out? Hmm, this is a tough one. Let's put it in perspective. If we say there are approximately 7.5 billion people on the planet and that each of them is having some sort of experience at all times, then what you are experiencing accounts for about .0000000133%, or thirteen millionth of a percent, of the experiences you could be having. So at any moment, you are missing 99.9999999867% of the possible experiences that are happening. In that case, you are always missing out on every other possible experience except for one. Well actually, by fearing missing out, you're missing out on that one, too.

By thinking about the other experiences you might be missing, it lends to you not being present, causing you to miss out on the only experience that you could actually be having at that moment. In that way, you create what you fear by fearing it. Embrace the moment you're in instead, and you can stop missing out on your life.

Fear of Change

Do you think you fear change? What specifically do you fear the changing of? You can't fear change itself because even as you read this your cells are changing. Your cells have already changed since you woke up this morning, and good thing they did, or you wouldn't be around very long. The sun came up, a pretty important change from last night's darkness.

Do you fear only unexpected change? If that's the case, would your fear disappear if you either expected change from now on or dropped your expectation entirely? Have you ever gotten a surprise gift or met someone new when you weren't expecting it? Did that make you fearful? If not, then it isn't the unexpected change as a whole that you fear. Maybe you fear your ability to adapt to change. Then again, if you are reading this right now, you've adapted from before you could read to be able to read. You probably also use a phone, the internet, and drive a car. All of these are demonstrations of your ability to adapt to change.

So I have to know, how sure are you that you do fear change? What if you don't? What if you actually love and embrace change, and you just forgot that somewhere along the way?

What if you actually love and embrace change, and you just forgot that somewhere along the way?

Reconstructing Your Empowered Self

While reframing, Cartesian Coordinates and other methods, work with the Unconscious Mind, sometimes a particular limiting belief or emotion won't release with those methods alone. There are also NLP (Neuro-Linguistic Programming) and MER® (Mental and Emotional Release®) techniques that can work more directly with the unconscious mind. For work with these techniques like Parts Integration, MER®, additional Quantum Linguistics, Prime Concerns, and others, find a Practitioner or Master Practitioner of NLP and/or MER®, or seek certification yourself. You can get connected with a Master Practitioner by emailing info@aiponline.org and find resources for certification through Empowerment, Inc.™ at nlp.com. I was personally trained and certified through Empowerment, Inc.™

We talked about the Puppet Master earlier. You were the puppet being jerked around by your strings. When using Reframing, MER®, and many of the NLP techniques, it became the equivalent of you being jerked around, looking over, and noticing a mirror.

You changed your relationship with the problem, and the problem loosened or disappeared.

You looked in the mirror and realized that you were the Puppet Master, or that there were no strings and you imagined them, or that the string attached to your elbow moved to your toe. You changed your relationship with the problem, and the problem loosened or disappeared. Let's not forget that when we talk about the problem, we are not referring to external events but to the relationship we have with these events.

What is really the problem? Everything has two parts. There's the external part: the person, the behavior of another person, or a certain situation. Then there's the internal part, which is your relationship to the external part. Your relationship to the 'external thing' is what we have the most control over. In that way, we have a tremendous amount of control over our experience of life. Viktor Frankl's quote from *Man's Search for Meaning* leads us in the right direction. "Everything can be taken from a man but one thing: the last of the human freedoms — to choose one's attitude in any given set of circumstances, to choose one's own way."

Let's delve a little deeper into what I believe Viktor is saying.

If we can always be in control of the attitude we hold, the meaning we give something, and what we're focused on, then we can shift those things at any time to better serve us. This shifts our entire experience.

Remember, how you relate to the problem is the problem. The way you see the problem is what's most important in determining how big of a problem it is or if it even is a problem. You can look at a situation in a way that makes a small problem become Mount Everest, and you can look at something in a way that makes the problem completely disappear or even become a positive thing. Think of this like the fun house mirrors. Your perception is the mirror that is stretching, shrinking, and influencing, and you have control over changing that mirror. You have the power.

Reinforcing Empowering Perceptions

We've examined changing your perception, limiting beliefs, and unwanted emotional states. As you do the work to change your perception, there is a lot of letting go of unwanted beliefs or emotions. Once the limiting ways you were perceiving it are gone, it's important to reinforce what you want instead. It's time to focus on what you do want and create positive habits around it. Visualization is one of the most underutilized tools in reinforcing what we want. The unconscious mind doesn't know the difference between vivid imagination and reality.

- Do you make a million dollars per year?

- Do you run a successful business with employees?

- Are you a professional athlete or musician?

- Have you helped provide a billion meals to those in need?

- Do you regularly speak in front of thousands of people?

Did the people that have achieved those things first achieve them and then see themselves as those things, or did they see themselves as those things and then achieve them? If you ask people with accomplishments at that level, almost all will tell you they would visualize it consistently before it actually happened.

Think of something you greatly desire that you haven't yet started believing you can accomplish. Without believing you can do it, what thoughts will you have about accomplishing it? Henry Ford is attributed with saying, "Whether you believe you can do a thing or not, you are right." Your actions will follow those thoughts and beliefs. The person who believes they can't do something isn't going to wake up excited each day and show up in a powerful way to accomplish it.

You might say that once you accomplish it, you'll believe yourself capable of it. So not only would you have to overcome all of the obstacles in your way, but you would also have to overcome yourself.

Instead, imagine you believe yourself capable of achieving your goal. You believe it to be an inevitability. You picture yourself already having accomplished it, and know it's just a matter of time. You close your eyes every night and you see yourself there. You can imagine the scenery and the smells, feel the texture and hear the sounds that make it real.

Now, what thoughts will you have? How will you wake up each morning? What actions will you take? You can choose to believe it or not. That's kind of the point. What do you have to lose? Better yet, how much do you have to gain?

Now that we have gone through the evolution from disempowered to empowerment, I want to sum up the shift in a simple story.

It happened again. They made me mad. I feel like a passenger on a hijacked train. My emotions are running me.

It happened again. They made me sad. I fought back and hurt them. They had no right to try and make me feel anything.

It happened again. They scared me. Technically, I scared me based on what they said. Feels a little less bad when I say it like that.

It happened again. I made myself feel guilty from what they said. But it wasn't really about me anyway. Maybe I'll not do that next time.

It happened again. That's all, a simple happening. And I left it there. What else would I like to focus on today instead?

Recommended Beliefs

To finish, I want to share a handful of beliefs that I recommend. These have helped me tremendously in my life, and I trust at least one of them will do the same for you.

- In any experience, there is always a positive lesson.

When I believe this, it causes me to search for the lesson and focus on the positive, no matter the situation. This isn't to say terrible things don't happen. They do. I've been knocked off my feet plenty of times by life, as we all have. This isn't just some trite 'everything happens for a reason' kind of belief. Two things can be true: Life can bring us tremendous challenges that feel unfair in the moment, and we can reframe those events to empower us in our journey forward, taking the positive lessons from the 'school of life' along with us.

- I can learn something from any person.

I mean anyone. A tiny infant, someone who is begging on the street corner, the president of a company, the person in line next to me at the coffee shop. This causes me to pay attention and look for the learnings. Wisdom often comes from unexpected sources.

- <u>Opportunities for learning are in every moment if I choose.</u>

Simply being aware of the world around me teaches me so much. There is as much to learn in a quiet moment alone on a porch when the world is still as there is in a 'TED talk' or in a classroom, if only I am paying attention to everything unfolding around me.

- <u>Strong opinions, loosely held.</u>

Always be open to the counterargument. I do my best not to identify with my opinions because if I do, it will cause me to hold on to them too tightly. Being wrong isn't that big of a deal because I value becoming more aware of what is true more than I value not being wrong.

- <u>"What is most personal is most universal." - Carl Rogers</u>

My deepest fears, what I'm most afraid for the world to see, those judging thoughts I'm ashamed of, and anything else found in the deep, dark recesses of my mind are what can cause me to feel alone in the world. They make me different. They isolate me.
Except they don't. Those are the exact things that surface time and time again when I work one-on-one with others. The question or statement is always the same, "Do other people ever share this kind of thing with you? I bet I'm the only one."
At that moment, it is like looking into the mirror and seeing myself and all of the other people I've worked with looking back at me through the same eyes. Those things exist within all of us. They are deeply personal and also universal. Our hiding them from the light and creating our own separateness create the real problem. When I have moments of feeling most alone, I remind myself that there is a world full of people feeling the same things at different times.

- <u>I do hard things just because they are hard sometimes.</u>

This one might seem odd on the surface, yet it creates further resilience within me and reminds me of what I am capable of. It also reframes other experiences in life to seem easier.

- <u>Nothing about tomorrow should ever take my focus away from today.</u>

Being present is a wonderful gift to everyone in my world and the greatest gift I can give them and myself. I can plan for tomorrow, be excited about the future, and then ground myself back into the present. Tomorrow only exists in my mind, for when it comes, it will simply be a uniquely different 'today'.

Tomorrow only exists in my mind, for when it comes, it will simply be a uniquely different 'today'.

- Everyone else is a human, too.

My teacher, my coach, the CEO of the company, the incredible speaker, the person who seems bulletproof? They are all exactly as human as I am. They all have harder days and easier days. They all have doubts and fears from time to time. They all have moments of indecision or second-guessing. "I could never be like them" doesn't exist in my mind because I already am like them, just with a different set of beliefs, thoughts, feelings, and habits.

It is a disservice to them and me to act like they are superhuman. Doing so creates an unbridgeable gap between myself and them because no matter how much I succeed, I will always be highly aware of my own shortcomings and fallible humanness.

- I strive to find things to appreciate about everything I do.

When I expect to find things to appreciate, they appear: The way the dishes stack in their proper places; the way my body holds me up twenty-five miles into a marathon; the way I get to look through a window into someone else's life when I work with them; the way I get to see a calm and quiet world when I wake up at 3am to catch a flight. I used to miss the beauty in all these things because I was too busy focusing on the negative. They are always there, just waiting for me to notice.

- Let go.

Finally, I'd like to let you into a type of conversation I have with myself often.

"I'm gripping life too tightly; let go a little. Let go of my attachment to reading a few more pages when the interruption comes. Let go of the fear of how tomorrow might be when I am able to get only half of the sleep I planned on tonight. Let go of the tension I'm holding when I realize there is a two-hour delay in my travel. Let go of the increasing pressure when three more urgent things come up on an already overbooked day. Let go, let go, let go."

I trust that your journey through this book and the exercises have added to your toolkit for life and been a net-positive experience for you. I hope you have gained as much by reading this book as I have by sharing it with you. This book is to be a tool for you.

Often, we read books for solutions and answers. We hope the author will give us something we don't have, assuming we don't already have the answers within us. I disagree with this premise. I believe the purpose of a book isn't to give us something we don't have. Instead, I believe the purpose of a book is to help us gain awareness of the resources available inside of us that have been there our whole life. My goal is not to give you the answers. My goal is to remind you how to ask the questions so you can get the best answers for your journey whenever you need them.

I hope this book has been an immersive experience, leaving you with something tangible you can integrate into your life.

In that spirit of tangible, visible progress, use the lines below right now to write the new beliefs and insights that can help you in your empowerment.

What are your takeaways from reading this book and doing the exercises?

_____

_____

_____

_____

_____

_____

_____

_____

_____

_____

_____

Acknowledgments

I come from a place of sincere gratitude and deep appreciation in thanking those who have helped me along my path so far. Some have lent a hand to pull me from the dark, some have given me a gut check, and many have given me guidance or assistance without even knowing it. I am a product of the environments I've been in, and I have had the privilege to be in incredible environments thus far.

I will inevitably miss giving gratitude to everyone who has positively influenced me, so to everyone who has contributed to the person I am becoming and has helped me be a resource for empowerment for others, I thank you with all of my heart.

To my coaches: To my first coach Jodi Vavricka: thank you for refusing to tolerate my excuses, for giving me the idea of becoming a coach, and for recommending "You Can Heal Your Life" by Louise Hay, which started my journey of inner self-exploration and healing. Thank you to Aaron Simons for the push in following through to become a coach and for guiding me in that process. Thank you to George Gillas for pulling back the curtain further on my relationship with myself and my values and for introducing me to NLP. Thank you to Rich Anderson for uncovering the journey back to my heart and reconnection with faith that was desperately needed. Thank you to John Vander Gheynst for furthering my understanding of how these wonderful tools can help others find their way to empowerment. Thank you to Craig Zuber for challenging me to step into my greatness and think at a level I didn't know existed.

Thank you to Dr. Matt James and Empowerment, Inc. for providing me with the resources to develop skills in NLP and MER® and showing me a path to much deeper work.

Thank you to all the teachers, sports coaches, and earliest

relationships that taught me valuable life lessons and helped develop my drive, empathy, humility, and personal power.

To the MAPS Coaching ecosystem, Dianna Kokoszka, Monica Reynolds, and all of my fellow coaches, for being the environment I needed to belong to right when I needed it most. To the Cadre group for challenging me to continually move toward my potential and for the accountability to a deadline on writing this book. To the Performance coaching group for facilitating a place where the depth of conversation lights up my soul.

To Tony Robbins, Anthony De Mello, Louise Hay, Dr. Matt James, Byron Katie, Brené Brown, David R. Hawkins, and all the authors of the many books that have helped in my development, for having the courage to follow through on the vulnerable journey of writing books that allowed me to be in close relationship with you.

To Monica, Jenny, Lisa, and the rest of the Taylor Team, for being a huge support for me so I can spend more time writing, coaching, and growing.

To all of the coaching clients I've had the privilege to partner with, for allowing me to walk alongside you and be a resource for you in your journey. Thank you for teaching and growing me. I hope that I have been able to give you at least a fraction of what you've given me in our partnerships.

To my brothers, Blair and Lance. To Blair, for being the pressure needed to create and uncover the power within myself. Thank you for being the iron to sharpen myself against, for believing in me long before I believed in myself, and for the unassuming moments of deep insight and wisdom. To Lance, for modeling and facilitating the kind of conversations that sparked my curiosity and desire to learn, grow, and uncover the depth of this experience of life.

To my parents, Tony and Susan, for raising me exactly how I needed to be to prepare me for my path. For always supporting my goals and dreams, and for dad being brave and humble enough to be my first coaching client. Thank you for showing me the world and how different and the same all of it can be simultaneously. Thank you for encouraging me to pursue my interests, supporting me in developing a wide array of unrelated talents, and ingraining in me one of the best rules in our household: Never quit something you've committed to.

To all of my friends and family, for tolerating my rigid schedule and compulsions to coach and dissect concepts and situations in my personal life, for occasionally allowing me to practice on them, and for being supportive as I change and grow. To Philip, for late-night conversations and being on the journey together during the chaotic transition from schooling to adulthood. To Brent, for the

Acknowledgments 135

ongoing support, the trips to Oxford, and the deep conversations that have etched themselves into the expression of who I am. To Haley, for being the ultimate role model for living a family-centric life. To Jody, for being a role model on how to slow down into life and get every last bit of enjoyment out of it.

To Mitzi Helmick, for giving me incredible feedback early in the process on the flow of my writing. To my editor, Jackie Buxton, for giving me thorough feedback even when it hurt, so that this book could clearly convey the message that was in my heart through the words on these pages. To Erica Ord, for your attention to detail regarding copyediting, grammar, and punctuation, I'm glad we handled those improper commas and dangling modifiers. To Angela Belford and The Belford Group, for the beautiful cover art, proper formatting and layout of the book, and guidance along the way.

To my children, Corilyn, Brighton, Brecken, and Layton, I want to express my gratitude for being a major source of inspiration in my journey to acquire the tools and skills needed to empower others. You have motivated me to document the knowledge and wisdom I gain so that I can help you achieve true empowerment at an early age in life.

Finally, to my wife, partner, best friend, and greatest support, Bryn. At least half of the good ideas I've had have come from you, and you graciously let me take credit for the other half simply because I've forgotten you said them first. Thank you for being a container big enough for my emotions, for holding space for me, for always believing in me, and for your incredible patience. Thank you for being an awe-inspiring example for me of how to love our children with all of your being. Thank you for listening to my processing of everything I learn and for acting interested when I explain the relationship between emotions and the unconscious mind, the holographic nature of reality, MER®, and any other "woo-woo" thing I come across.

Tools/Questions/ Exercises From the Book

This section includes the tools, questions, and exercises we've used throughout the book. It is meant as a quick-reference guide to come back to as you uncover beliefs, thoughts, or emotions that surface for resolution.

Cartesian Coordinates
What do you gain by _____?
What do you gain by not _____?
What do you lose by _____?
What do you lose by not _____?

Actions vs. Intentions
- Think back to the last three times you were hurt, upset, or frustrated by someone else. Write them down.

- Write what their positive intention might have been.

- Put it all together in this format:

- "The way they attempted to express (positive intention) was (the action they took). They were taking the best approach to getting (positive intention) that they knew at the time."

Person vs. Object
- Think about three situations in the past week where you may have treated a person as an object. Write them down if that's helpful.

- Next, write down a potential backstory to humanize these people.

- Now, write how you would have treated them instead, had you been conscious of that backstory while you were interacting with them.

Environment (Childhood Influences)
- What was your environment like when you were very young?

- What positive and negative associations did you make based on that environment?

- Was there stability in your household?

- How did you need to behave to be safe or to receive love?

- What did you need to do to get attention from your parents?

- How did you have to act to get what you wanted?

- What behaviors were rewarded? What behaviors were punished?

- Did you receive more attention for things you did well or things you didn't do well?

- How was expressing emotion modeled for you?

- Were you allowed to have problems as a child?

- How were you responded to when you expressed emotions?

- If you had siblings, what was your role (caretaker, baby of the family, etc)?

- What was your role with your parents (always needed their help, allowed to be a carefree child, needed to fix everything so they wouldn't get upset)?

The Shadow
- Write the things that are 'not you'. Example: "I am never dishonest."

- Write out something negative that you consistently experience. Maybe it is that everyone in your world is dishonest with you. Maybe they are constantly pushy. Maybe a lot of people in your world are selfish. Write these out. For example: "Others consistently lie to me or deceive me."

- Take everything you wrote down and do some soul-searching. Assume for a moment that your unconscious mind is hiding from you the ways in which you are the way you said you aren't or that you are guilty of the thing that you believe everyone else is doing.

- Write out the examples in the form of "I" statements.

The Escalator
- Write out the situations or common occurrences in your life where you feel unconscious resistance. Leave space after each for the next part of the exercise.

- Now, go back to what you wrote and write next to them both the intention for your conscious and your unconscious mind.

- Rewrite your statements in a "this action means this" or "this action will cause this" form.

- Pull the limiting belief from each statement.

- Run each limiting belief, one at a time, through these 2 sets of questions:

"It's a good thing to not know" by Dr. Matt James'

What is it?

What is it not?

How do you know what it is not?

What do you need to not know to know this?

Your Relationship with Life

- Use the left-hand page to write the story of your life. Write it in the form of life happening to you. Allow yourself to focus on the tougher experiences you've had. Write them all down in chronological order as best you can. Start from as far back as you can remember. This is the time to get all of it out into the open. Be completely transparent with yourself. Write about the events of hurt and shame. Write about the pain and the heartbreak. Write about your missteps and failures. Do not filter; allow it all out onto the page. Take the time, now, to write it.

- Write the story of your life again on the right-hand page. This time, write all of it from the viewpoint of life happening for you. Reference that section from Mary above as needed to hold that perspective. Write about all the things that happened in your life up to this point as if they are the ingredients that have made you who you are and the stepping stones that have prepared you for what's next.

Values

- What is important to you about [a romantic relationship]?

- Write out your definition of the word you wrote above (or said to yourself):

- What has to happen for your value of [trust] to be violated in a relationship?

- How do you know when your value of [trust] is being met in a relationship?

What-Ifs

- Write out all the negative 'what-ifs' on your mind.

- Mark them out and rewrite them as positive 'what-ifs.'

Positively Influencing Our Emotional State

- Use the blank diagram or draw a copy of it.

- Fill in the original event information from a recent experience that ended in a negative emotional state or response.

- Put the same event in the "Positive Alternative" box, then add other possible positive meanings in the "Meaning" box. If you can't find any, phone a friend. Because, you know, we can always find a positive meaning.

- Finally, write out the appropriate experience, emotional state, or response based on the meaning you gave it.

- Reach up really high with one hand, bend your arm at the elbow, and pat yourself on the back, you have just empowered yourself by creating a positive experience out of what used to be a negative experience.

Rinse and repeat as many times as you'd like to feel more empowered.

The Chicken and the Egg

"When I have the right mindset, I do the activity."
- Take an area in your life where you believe this is true. One possibility is, "when I feel motivated to work out, I go to the gym and work out."

- Now, reverse the sentence. "When I go to the gym and work out, I feel motivated to work out."

- Is it also true? If so, celebrate.

Reframing
- Go back to this exercise of "Your Relationship With Life", take a few of your responses, and write them again here. Write down the 3 most painful things that have happened to you in your life.

- As we know, there is great power in our darkest moments if we choose to use them for our empowerment and write the positive reframe of them. Rewrite your three things in an empowering way.

Proving the impossible possible
- What is impossible for you? Write out everything you can think of that is impossible for you.

- Order them from 'most impossible' to 'just beyond possible'.

Cartesian Coordinates
Take a limiting belief and run it through these 4 questions.

*What would happen if you did?

_____

*What wouldn't happen if you did?

_____

*What would happen if you didn't?

_____

*What wouldn't happen if you didn't?

_____

www.ingramcontent.com/pod-product-compliance
Lightning Source LLC
Chambersburg PA
CBHW051529120626
46551CB00012B/1145